MY PERFECT PLACE IN IRELAND

MY PERFECT PLACE IN IRELAND

Irish Personalities Share Their Most-loved Locations

Róisín Ingle

BLACK & WHITE PUBLISHING

First published in the UK in 2022 by
Black & White Publishing Ltd
Nautical House, 104 Commercial Street, Edinburgh, EH6 6NF

A division of Bonnier Books UK
4th Floor, Victoria House, Bloomsbury Square, London, WC1B 4DA
Owned by Bonnier Books
Sveavägen 56, Stockholm, Sweden

A CIP catalogue record for this book is available from the British Library.

ISBN: 978 1 78530 430 9

1 3 5 7 9 10 8 6 4 2

Layout by creativelink.tv
Printed and bound in Great Britain by Bell & Bain Ltd, Glasgow

www.blackandwhitepublishing.com

To all the places and people that
nurture our mental health . . .

CONTENTS

ABOUT
A LUST FOR LIFE

By buying or reading this book you are supporting A Lust for Life, a multi-award-winning mental health charity based in Ireland. We use content, campaigning and events to remove stigma and encourage young people to be effective guardians of their own mental health.

The "A Lust for Life Schools" programme is rooted in mindfulness and education. Since 2020, the initiative has been delivered in Irish classrooms to over 33,000 children, helping to raise emotional resilience and awareness in people from the earliest possible age. Anchored in leading psychological and pedagogical practices and featuring a Netflix-style platform where teachers and children can access mental wellbeing content in a fun and scalable way, the programme includes teacher-led lesson plans, activities and resources to bring the digital content to life.

A Lust for Life also aims to facilitate future generations to lead, connect and learn through content and campaigns inspired and curated by them. Building on this principle, the charity is currently piloting their "Gone Past Talking" programme aimed at Transition Year students across Ireland. Through this project, we provide young people with a toolkit to effectively manage and talk about their own minds.

Getting young people involved in tackling social challenges in their communities and the world has a profoundly positive impact on their mental and emotional wellbeing. Alongside instilling a positive sense of purpose, connection and identity, it also creates change-makers in every part of Ireland, who maintain and influence the country they want to inherit.

We are grateful to you, the reader, for supporting this book and we hope reading it empowers you to have conversations about mental health, leading you on a journey to find your own perfect places.

FOREWORD

PERFECTION is in the eye of the beholder. That's one thing I discovered while talking to people for this book about perfect places in Ireland. And something else that became clear: these beloved Irish locations are as much about family and friendship and childhood and sense memory and a tender sort of eulogising of the past as they are about geography.

An actor's appreciation for a panoramic Antrim coast view is made more meaningful when gazed upon from a deckchair in a close friend's garden. A writer's gritty Dublin council estate conjures up memories of the characters and capers from an adventure-filled childhood. A singer's fondness for a stunningly situated Donegal golf course is revealed, at heart, to be a family saga going back generations. And all of these perfect places are as vivid in the minds of those who love them as they are on any map.

It's also clear that there is no definitive recipe for treasured places. But the same ingredients do come up in conversation time and time again: a pinch of geographical beauty, a dollop of historical interest and a generous serving of emotional connection, often linked to childhood nostalgia.

From a lakeside revelation in Galway to the late discovery of a Dublin mountain, from family fun in a coastal Co. Kerry town to a fascination for the sheep-grazed ruins of a castle in Co. Antrim, and from a family escape to a grand country home in Co. Laois to a courageous activist finding solace in a bustling park in the centre of our capital city, this book is full of stories about glorious or ordinary, sometimes gloriously ordinary, places in Ireland.

I hope this book might inspire you to seek out these locations yourself and encourage you to reflect on your own perfect places in Ireland, wherever you may find them.

— Róisín Ingle, Dublin

NIALL BRESLIN
THE LAKES OF MULLINGAR

NIALL BRESLIN is a mental health advocate, former rugby player, best-selling author and chart-topping singer-songwriter with power-punk band The Blizzards. As co-founder and Creative Director of A Lust for Life, Niall's own experience has informed his journey to becoming a leading figure in mindfulness for individuals and organisations. His work has led to numerous awards including the prestigious Social Entrepreneur Ireland Impact award and the Google Impact Award amongst others.

There are three major lakes around the Westmeath town of Mullingar: Loch Ainninn, Loch Uail and Loch Dairbhreach. The lakes attract plenty of visitors for swimming, boating and fishing – they are famous for an abundance of pike and trout. Close to Loch Ainninn is Lilliput, the place that inspired *Gulliver's Travels* by Jonathan Swift. A regular visitor to the area, Swift is said to have been on a boat in the lake when he looked back and saw how small people appeared from a distance. For Mullingar man Niall Breslin, these midlands lakes have always been his perfect place . . .

The lakes around Westmeath and my hometown of Mullingar are some of the most beautiful places in Ireland and nobody knows about them. It's just never mentioned in the tourism brochures or the campaigns. Part of me feels that it's very strange and another part of me feels quite happy about that. Like, let's keep it under wraps so nobody ever finds out.

I've been utterly obsessed with the lakes since I was a child, particularly Loch Ainninn but Loch Uail as well. It's no exaggeration to say the lakes of Westmeath and Mullingar have been a mental life jacket for me so many times.

I started cycling out there on my own or with mates from about the age of thirteen, it's a twenty-minute bike ride from my family home in Mullingar. Every time something goes wrong I always end up at Loch Ainninn. When Kurt Cobain died in 1994 three of us cycled out to the lake, like we were in some kind of cheesy 1980s movie. We stood by the lake feeling confused, scared and listening to Nirvana songs. Our hero just died and no one

"It's no exaggeration to say the lakes of Westmeath and Mullingar have been a mental life jacket for me so many times."

would talk to us about it. We didn't really know why, but I do now.

It's funny that I have a thing for the lakes because I've had a deep fear of water and fish since I was a child. I'd stare at the lakes all day no problem but you'd never have gotten me into one. For a long time I hated the idea of swimming in open water, rivers, seas or lakes. And even more than the water, I was appalled at the thought of being around fish and these lakes are full of pike and trout.

One year I decided to face my fear. I signed up to do a triathlon even though I couldn't swim and detested the thought of both fish and water. When I started lake swimming, everything changed. My first open water swim was in Loch Uail. I couldn't sleep properly for a week before the swim but it was such an incredibly positive experience that I got into the lake every day for months afterwards. I spent the entire pandemic in Mullingar and swam there every day. It's difficult to describe but swimming there feels like you are giving the lake everything. All your problems. All your worries. It helps that the water is clean and clear, because it's fed by a spring.

A friend of mine also had a fear of fish and water so after I got sorted I brought him to the lake to try and help him get over his phobia. I don't know what happened that day but there were so many fish around you could hardly see the water and he was terrified. He's never been in the water since, he can barely take a bath now. So, the lake cure doesn't work for everyone. But for me the lakes of Mullingar have been and always will be the greatest therapy.

I was home last week, my head was fried, I just went out there and immediately felt better. I can't explain it, there is just something about that place. I've looked into this a bit. The gentle movement of lake water is at a frequency of about 430 hertz, so it's much quieter than the sea. That quiet movement of the lake does something for me, sets off something in my head. Everyone needs a place that makes you feel like you don't have to keep up with the world and that's the lakes for me. There is something about nature that we are hardwired for. The modern world has conditioned us to be mindless, it doesn't want us to just be present but when we are present, at least for those moments, everything feels okay.

"Everyone needs a place that
makes you feel like you don't
have to keep up with the world."

Loch Uail is the more aesthetically pleasing of the two lakes I tend to visit – it's just visually stunning. It's harder to get to my favourite spot by Loch Ainninn, you have to walk through a little forest. While it might not be quite as beautiful as Loch Uail, I love it because it's just really wild, you could be in Canada. It's a pain in the hoop to get to and that's why you won't see many people around. It's the smell of the place I love, the scent of bamboo I think, and the silence and the sounds of nature.

I can't stay at the lakes for very long, mind you. I am not some guy who can sit there for hours and eat twigs and hug trees. That's not what I do. A half-hour away from the world is enough for me and it has been since I was a child. It's had a hugely positive influence on my mental health. I've moved away from home now. I bought my first house in Co. Wicklow, which is one of the most beautiful places in the world. But my dream is always to live by the lakes in Mullingar. And I hope it will happen someday.

LIZ NUGENT
TYRONE GUTHRIE CENTRE

LIZ NUGENT is a bestselling Irish crime writer. Born in Dublin in 1967, she has spent the last twenty years working in Irish film, theatre and television. Her first novels, *Unravelling Oliver*, *Lying in Wait* and *Skin Deep*, have all gained her Irish Book Awards and become number-one bestsellers, whilst her latest novel *Our Little Cruelties* was listed by *The New York Times* as a recommended thriller for 2020. Aside from writing, Liz has led workshops in writing drama for broadcast and interviewed many notable figures including Joseph O'Connor, Sinead Crowley and Graham Norton.

Theatre director Tyrone Guthrie was raised at Annaghmakerrig and bequeathed the house and lands to the Irish State as a residential facility for creative artists. Founded in 1981, the Arts Council-supported Tyrone Guthrie Centre is a place of contemplation, creativity and collaboration. For decades now, Irish and international writers and artists of all disciplines have made art in quiet solitude joining other artists each evening at 7pm for a communal dinner in what is affectionately known as the 'Big House'. For Liz Nugent, Annaghmakerrig is her perfect place . . .

Some writers of commercial fiction think they can't go to Annaghmakerrig, that you have to be a literary writer to go there, but that is just not true. The first time I applied, I had only written one piece for RTE's *Sunday Miscellany*, a story about a pair of exquisitely beautiful gloves I saw in the window of a shop one day. It took me several more years to summon the courage to audaciously apply for a week-long residency. In my application I said I'd written a *Sunday Miscellany* and that I'd like to write a book.

I couldn't believe I got accepted. I was quite scared the first time I went there in 2010. Somebody had told me the place was notorious, a virtual knocking shop so I had visions of all these artists and writers in and out of each other's bedrooms. Now, it's true that a lot of people have met their partners there – the last time I stayed I met one couple who met there thirty-five years ago – but I needn't have worried,

"Whatever you can do or
dream you can, begin it;
Boldness has genius,
power, and magic in it."

"The grounds are stunning, but it's really the people who work there that make the place what it is."

even though I did keep my bedroom door locked that first time.

There's the Big House on top of a hill where I usually stay and behind it are the visual art studios and several self-catering cottages for those who don't want to stay in the house. The house is on 450 acres of mature woodland, overlooking the sweeping lawn down to a lake where masochists dive in for a swim in winter and summer. I've never been one of those people. But the place is so calm, so peaceful and so beautiful, the perfect place for creativity.

Everything at Annaghmakerrig is geared around making life comfortable and productive for the artists. There is only one rule if you are staying in the house: you must join the other residents for dinner each evening. That first night around the dinner table I hardly said anything, I was a bit intimidated. What I realised very quickly was that you didn't have to be a known writer or a celebrity to be there. I didn't know anybody around the table. The place is such a leveller. It was a hugely diverse bunch but everybody has one really important thing in common: they are all there to do their work. Nobody asks you for your CV when you are sitting around the table at dinner. People might ask, "How did you get on with your work today?" but even that question can be fraught if the day hasn't gone as well as some people might have hoped. I asked that question of an American writer one time and he said, "Work? I'm a poet." Which was great because it made me think that what I was doing didn't have to be work, that it could be a pleasure. But to this day I still haven't learned how to enjoy writing, I still find it incredibly hard work. I wish I enjoyed working as much as some other people.

I worked so hard there that first year – I've never worked as hard there since, I think I wrote 12,000 words in a week, which is a huge output for me. I wrote like a demon. Back then there was no Wi-Fi in the bedrooms, which helped. I was working on expanding a short story into my first novel *Unravelling Oliver*.

It felt like I was living that Goethe quote, "Whatever you can do or dream you can, begin it; Boldness has genius, power, and magic in it." I just decided to do it, to write my novel, and Annaghmakerrig was the perfect place to begin.

I won a bursary a couple of years later to spend two weeks there. The grounds are stunning, but it's really the people who work there that make the place what it is. There is no us and them. The staff are such a part of all that is achieved there because they make everything so beautiful for the residents. They put flowers on the table at dinnertime. Freshly baked scones appear at 11am.

It's in the countryside, so there's never a dull moment. Sometimes a bat will fly in a window and cause hysteria in the house. And in the winter there's a constant battle with mice which the staff always win. And people will tell you lots of stories about the mysteries of the house and how it's haunted, but I've never seen any of the ghosts myself.

I'm so grateful for Annaghmakerrig. It's where I do my best work. It's a place that makes sense for me and for so many artists. You don't have to do your laundry or worry what you are having for dinner or be concerned about any of the life tasks that get in the way of writing. It's just silence, creative camaraderie and the swans on the lake.

DARA Ó BRIAIN

VICAR STREET, DUBLIN

DARA Ó BRIAIN is a hugely popular stand-up comedian and TV presenter from Bray, Co Wicklow. Ó Briain's TV work includes hosting programmes such as *Mock the Week*, *Robot Wars* and *Three Men in a Boat*. Dara has performed shows all over world, from Moscow to Sydney, Tromsø to Malta, and has captivated audiences over 200 times at Dublin's legendary Vicar Street.

Owned by Harry Crosbie, Vicar Street opened in Dublin in 1998 as a concert and events venue. It has the capacity to seat 1,050 people or 1,500 standing in the main venue. Over the years some huge names in music and comedy have played in that room, including Dara Ó Briain. Of all the venues he's played in the world, Vicar Street is his perfect room . . .

There's a lovely moment during a Vicar Street show when I ask the audience, "Hey, who is here from outside of Ireland?" and there's usually a small number of people who have travelled from other countries. I always assume they are there because I keep banging on about how brilliant Vicar Street is when I do international shows. When these people make themselves known, the audience all get a bit "oh they've come to this venue especially to see us, so we should also perform" and it adds to the atmosphere.

I tend to mythologise theatres a lot. I'm really into theatre design and particularly fond of the Frank Matcham style which emerged at the end of the Victorian age. You know the ones, red velvet seats, three levels. Stalls, circle, grand circle. That design is by some distance the best theatre design of all. But we forgot how to do it and we started building these black boxes where you are on the same level as the people in the front seats. It's not right. You should be looking up at your audience, there's a physics to it all.

Even though Vicar Street bucks that trend of looking up at your audience it's still the perfect place for what I do. There are some elemental things: it's a square room. The bar is outside. And it's relatively intimate, wide as opposed to long, so you feel a connection, as though you could reach out and touch the audience.

The other thing that you won't find anywhere else is that the audience are seated on tiny stools around little tables. You might wonder why anyone would design a venue with tiny stools for the audience. But it works. It means they can drink, which makes it more informal, and they are in groups, which makes it very relaxed.

In other venues, lovely warm rooms with plush chairs, the audience are sunk into the seats and it does take the edge off their reaction. People are more passive in those seating situations. It's kind of like, "here we are now, entertain us" instead of them feeling like they are going to be involved. In Vicar Street, people are more ready to go, they are literally on the edge of their seats.

American TV chat-show host David Letterman used to do a trick where he'd make sure the audience were cold, so they never dozed off or got sleepy during a show. The ironically named warm-up man would tell audience members to take off their coats because they looked bad on camera. So the audience would sit there shivering. I think that's a bit extreme, but the tiny stools do seem to bring an informality to the situation which works very well for us performers.

There are other things unique to the place. The staff are exceptional. If I come up with a silly idea, from a chat I've been having with the audience during a show, they'll always facilitate me. One time, I was having banter with a man who said he played soccer for a league of Ireland team. During the interval the security guys went around to the flats behind Vicar Street until they found someone they could pay a fiver for a ball. Then in the second half I got your man up to test his football skills. The staff have done loads of things for me like that over the years.

The other aspect that makes it unique is the fact that Vicar Street is very loosely booked. Venues in London are often booked out solidly for months because of financial concerns and high theatre rents. Back in the day, when I was gaining momentum as a stand-up comic, I'd book a few nights and then they'd be able to say, we have another couple of nights next month, will you do them? So especially when you are starting to build your audience, you can find out what your level is. Am I a thousand-seater person? Am I an eight-thousand-seater person? No other venue books acts that way. I remember going from one night to eight nights, from fourteen to forty. It's all built up by word of mouth and facilitated by this looser booking situation at Vicar Street. We all enjoyed watching it happen with Joanne McNally. When the Vicar Street ball starts rolling it's an amazing thing to see.

The staff like to remind me of one of my first gigs there. It was during a tour I did in 2003, when everything went wrong in venues all over the country. I was playing to tiny audiences or sometimes I'd show up and the venue would be double-booked for a local fashion show. My night in Vicar Street was supposed to be the big culmination of the tour. That night

“There are times I come out of Vicar Street after a performance when I am so full of adrenaline I skip and dance and swing around lampposts on the walk back to the hotel.”

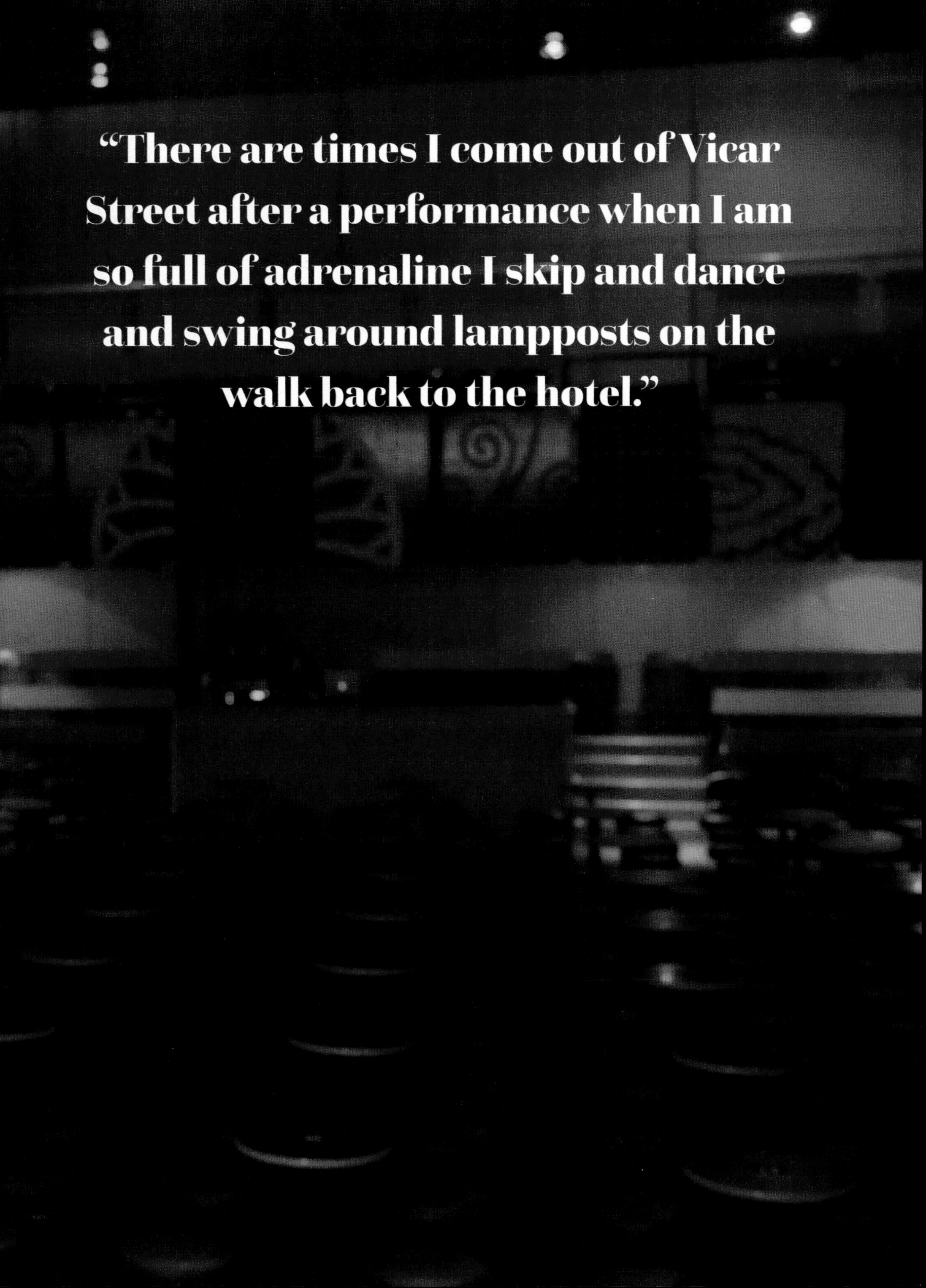

VICAR ST.
DUBLIN
VICAR ST.

Après Match had sold out the big room, the main venue, and I was doing my gig in the much smaller bar. But only thirty people showed up.

My year is always planned around Vicar Street even though I could schedule it differently. Instead of doing forty nights in Vicar Street over three seasons, you could do five or six nights in a big arena. But that would defeat the purpose. I love having so many legitimate reasons to come to Dublin and catch up with all my friends. They'll come to the shows or I'll see them afterwards. Even though I live in London, between the gigs at Vicar Street and my essential attendance at hurling matches, I've been able to keep in touch with all my friends in a way that I can justify to my wife.

I've spent far too much time in the back-stage bar at Vicar Street over the years. I had my fortieth birthday there, and my twenty-year school reunion. I wasn't sure if inviting my whole class to see me in a show was a dick move, but it ended up being an incredible night. They kept the bar open for us after and there's a photo I quite treasure of the last stragglers outside Vicar Street, at some mad hour of the morning. It's bright outside and we're all beaming at the camera, delighted. In the background you can see Jake, the head of security – who had to stay until we were all gone – just staring, looking slightly less happy.

There are times I come out of Vicar Street after a performance when I am so full of adrenaline I skip and dance and swing around lampposts on the walk back to the hotel. I'm acutely aware that my being on that stage is entirely dependent on the generosity of others. At some point there won't be forty nights for me to do, or ten nights or four nights. That's just the way it works. I've done over two hundred Vicars. I know I am not going to get to do another two hundred. I am aware of the dying of the light. At some point you just won't get the audiences, people will go to see someone else, someone younger.

The glorious privilege of playing this perfect room will not last forever. There's a photograph of Barcelona midfielder Andrés Iniesta lying on the pitch in the

"Even though Vicar Street bucks that trend of looking up at your audience it's still the perfect place for what I do."

stadium, the lights almost out, after he has played his last match. Tragically, that will be me when I do my last Vicar Street. I like an empty theatre: you can hear the old echoes of all the shows.

But when Vicar Street empties for my last show, I'll be weeping, lying down in the middle of the stage. They'll have to carry me out of the place.

JOHN LEGEND
VICAR ST
NOV. '04
In Person
BOB DYLAN
AND his BAND
'00
DARA
O BRIAIN
"A MASTERCLASS IN STAND-UP" -THE GUARDIAN
"HIS BREATHLESS SHOWS KEEP GETTING BETTER AND BETTER" -THE OBSERVER
Vicar
AL GREEN
SHOP
JUSTIN
"ONE OF THE MOST INFLUENTIAL POP COMPOSERS OF THE LAST 50 YEARS"
Brian Wilson
2005

RÓISÍN INGLE
ROUNDWOOD HOUSE, CO. LAOIS

RÓISÍN INGLE is a writer, journalist, podcaster and columnist for *The Irish Times*. Her popular weekly columns have been collected in two books, *Pieces of Me* and *Public Displays of Emotion*, and alongside Natasha Fennell, she is the author of *The Daughterhood*, an Irish bestseller which explores daughter-mother relationships. She is also co-presenter and producer of the award-winning *Women's Podcast*.

Located at the foot of the Slieve Bloom mountains in Mountrath, Co. Laois, Roundwood House is a country house hotel run by Hannah and Paddy Flynn. The couple live there with their two children, Amélie and Lucie, and several doted-upon animals. The main house, which has six guest bedrooms, is a fine example of Georgian architecture, built in 1741 by Anthony Sharp. It was boarded up and neglected for decades before being lovingly restored by the Irish Georgian Society. This is a home full of stories, songs, family and friendship. It's Róisín Ingle's perfect place . . .

Linda the robotic lawnmower has seen it all. She traverses the extensive lawns surrounding Roundwood House, impervious to the comings and goings of visitors. She's part of the electric and eclectic welcome committee that greets us every time we turn into the rambling drive of the Georgian manor in Co. Laois. Linda hums gently, going about her grass-cutting labour. A pair of geese, Mary and Jemima, peck around the cobbled yard honking territorially. There is a dog running about, of course. Penny was rescued having been abandoned during lockdown when she was just a tiny pandemic pup. Also roaming the yard are a couple of cats, some guinea fowl, a few ducks and any number of clucking hens. Two girls, Amélie and Lucie, emerge from the house full of chatter and smiles and hugs. At last, we're home.

Sort of. Our *actual* home is a small, terraced house in the north-inner city of

Dublin, an hour and twenty minutes from Roundwood House. There are no manicured-by-Linda lawns to be seen there, only a tiny yarden. No menagerie to speak of unless you count our elderly goldfish, Perry. But over the years, we've come to feel that as soon as we walk through the door of Roundwood House, sink into the sofa cushions in the drawing room, take that first bite of homemade flapjack and warm up by the fire, we are as much a part of this gracious home-from-home as the elegantly faded furniture.

Hannah Flynn, who makes those tasty flapjacks, grew up here with her five siblings and now runs Roundwood House with her Canadian-Irish husband, singer-songwriter and chef Paddy. Hannah's parents, Frank and Rosemarie Kennan, bought it in the 1980s from the Irish Georgian Society, which had lovingly restored the house after it lay neglected for decades. The walls are full of art and secrets, the furniture full of stories. In the drawing room there's a nearly two-hundred-year-old John Broadwood square piano. Open it up and you'll find a letter from Pigott and Co in Dublin dated 1947 explaining that the necessary repairs were deemed too expensive to complete. The carefully curated furnishings and art allow guests to play at living life in more refined times while taking advantage of all the possible mod cons.

We try our best to stay a few times each year. My favourite is our annual visit with a group of friends in deepest winter. We usually arrive on New Year's Day, Elish and Gerry, Susan and Trevor, myself and my partner Jonny, and all our children. There are epic games of hide and seek, and even more legendary games of Scrabble. The house is surrounded by eighteen acres of woodland, full in the spring and summer with bluebells and foxgloves and wild fuschia. For the more energetic there are gentle nature walks around the ground's perimeter and more challenging treks in the foothills and further reaches of the Slieve Bloom mountain range.

Each evening, Paddy cooks sumptuous four-course meals and dinner is eaten communally with other guests. Strangers bond over the cheese board, clashing occasionally when the conversation turns to politics. Breakfast, cooked by Hannah, is exceptional, with griddled scones and bacon beyond compare.

"The walls are full of art and secrets, the furniture full of stories."

NO BOOK IS TO BE TAKEN OUT
FOR WE HAVE SWORN AN OATH

Desmond Guinness, co-founder of the Irish Georgian society, once described Roundwood House as having "a dolls' house like quality". Standing outside the steel grey Palladian style building you can see his point. The front door is small and the windows narrow on each side. Once inside the doll's house, the double height hall comes as a surprise while the balustrades, with their ornate fretwork, would not look out of place in the grand circle of a theatre.

On those first days of each new year, in the glow of the lights from an enormous Christmas tree, the children make judicious use of this theatrical space. An audience of adults sits in rows on the central staircase, while the children use the grand hall as a stage from which to perform a variety show they've been rehearsing all day. There'll be a piano recital and maybe a bit of stand-up comedy. Somebody will sing like an angel. At one point nerves will scupper a performance or an acrobatic stunt will go hilariously wrong. The show often ends with both audience and performers joining together for a brief disco dancing moment. The children are teenagers now so those variety show days may well be gone forever. Still, we'll always have the memories and the incriminating photographs.

When it's time for an escape, there's the library. Hannah's dad Frank has collected books for years and 2,000 of them line the shelves in a beautifully converted barn at the back of the main house. This is Frank's Library, which contains books on

“It’s a haven. A hideaway.
A place to enjoy and appreciate
the best things in life.”

SCRABBLE
BALLYFIN

the theme of the evolution of civilisation. In his own words: "We need to be able to sit down and say that this room is as near as we can get to expressing where we are and how we got here. We need the warmth, beauty, excitement and tranquility of a library."

We might play a game of Bananagrams here in the afternoon, or amble over alone to relax and browse the books without any plan (or browse with intent – my friend Gerry always gravitates to a book of historic erotica, a tome he has nicknamed *Frank's Book of Antiquarian Dirty Pictures*). The library is also where you might find us all, wine glasses in hand, singing our hearts out in the smallest hours.

There is an indefinable magic about what Paddy and Hannah have achieved in this house which offers so much more than a typical hotel stay. Any visit is enhanced by chats with Amélie and Lucie about, say, their Abyssinian long-haired guinea pigs or made richer by Paddy's guitar interludes. He has an impressive song repertoire ranging from David Bowie to The Cure, Ron Sexsmith to Arcade Fire, not forgetting his own back catalogue of original songs.

I discovered recently that in the 1600s the grandfather of Anthony Sharp, who built Roundwood House, came to the area and purchased a property before establishing a small Quaker community named Friendstown. The spirit of Friendstown is still very much alive around these parts. Paddy and Hannah and their daughters have become dear friends. Even their official Twitter page explains that going there is "like visiting an old friend, who makes an occasion of a meal, warms you up by the fire and then charges you for it." Friendstown with benefits.

Roundwood House is a guest house, yes, but so much more than that. It's a haven. A hideaway. A place to enjoy and appreciate the best things in life, whether you fancy some relaxing solitude or noisy fun. Most importantly it's a home. In the blog he occasionally writes about Roundwood House, Paddy has confessed that when they first took it over, he was concerned about how the family would balance their private lives with the demands of the visiting public. Inevitably, adjustments were made. He and Hannah have become experts at having full-blown arguments using only their eyes. And sadly they had to cancel "Naked Tuesdays".

Over the years, through hosting all the wedding receptions and family reunions, team building weekends and anniversary dinners, romantic getaways and boisterous friend gatherings, the family learned how to wear this magnificent home comfortably, sharing its warmth with others. I'm so grateful that every once in a while we get to spend time with them all in this truly idyllic place.

DANIEL O'DONNELL

CRUIT ISLAND GOLF CLUB

DANIEL O' DONNELL is a household name in Ireland and Britain, known for his musical talent, philanthropy and charisma on stage and screen. Raised in the village of Kincasslagh, Daniel found fame after his first single "My Donegal Shore". Among many other achievements, Daniel was awarded an MBE in 2002 and became the first artist to have charted at least one new album in the UK charts for 28 consecutive years (1988–2015), selling over 10 million albums internationally.

The golf course at Cruit Island, perched on the edge of the Atlantic Ocean in Co. Donegal, has been described as a "dream place" by lovers of the sport. The nine-hole course is surrounded by the ocean, rugged rocks on all sides and is joined to the nearby village of Cionn Caslach (or Kincasslagh) by a bridge. Enthusiastic golfer Daniel O'Donnell knows the place well, having grown up around what he says is his perfect place . . .

Before there was ever a beautiful golf course here, this was the place I used to stand as a small child, looking out at all the islands. You can see Tory, Gola, Aran Mor and of course Owey Island, which is where my mother was born in 1919.

Owey Island is only five minutes in a boat from Cruit, so it's very close. Years ago there were no telephones, so to organise visits from friends and relatives, every house on Owey had a spot on the mainland. They called it a mark, and the marks were right in front of where the clubhouse now stands.

When I was a child, in the late 1960s, I'd go down and stand on my uncle's mark and someone on Owey Island would see that there was a person standing there. They'd go into my Uncle James's house or into my granny and say, "There's somebody on your mark, you better go out." And then my uncle would put the currach in the water and row over, not knowing

"Whether on a clear day or
in the middle of a storm, it
is simply magnificent."

"Every tee has an ocean view and it's like heaven on earth to play there."

who it was that wanted to come out to visit. There were no identifying features on each mark, everybody on the island just knew which one belonged to which house. It's amazing really when you think about how people organised themselves back then.

That stretch of water at the end of Cruit is called the sound. When my mother died, we were in the funeral home and my brother James suggested we should take her down to the sound one last time. So we brought my mother on tour in the hearse. When we pulled up in the hearse, the oldest person alive from Owey Island, a man called Neil Gallagher, said, "Take her up to her mark." He came out and showed us where the mark used to be, so we drove the hearse there, as if she was making her last journey home.

When I remember this place as a child it was a beautiful wilderness and it's still stunning now that the golf course is there. Every tee has an ocean view and it's like heaven on earth to play there. When I'm playing golf there now, for a lot of the time I'm looking out on Owey and on a good day you'll see Tory a long way off and Gola is a bit to the right. You see Carrickfinn beach and Gweedore and the Bloody Foreland all away ahead of you. When you stand up on the first tee, Arranmore is at your back and when you go over the hill on the third, the majesty of Errigal mountain is all in front of you. The mountain just seems to be in charge of everything. Now, there are days up there when you'd nearly need stones in your pockets to keep yourself from blowing away but whether on a clear day or in the middle of a storm, it is simply magnificent.

I've been playing golf there since 1997. I'm not very good. I play with friends and we always play for a little bit of money. You have to have a pound or two on it, or a few euro to keep the head down. My handicap is very high at the moment but I'm working on it. It's not a long course, but it's not easy either. It's definitely challenging. There are only two holes that let you see the flag when you are playing on the tee. The other seven holes are completely blind. If you can play Cruit golf course, you can lift your head and your bag and play anywhere in the world.

The sixth hole is a par three. It's up there with the best. How wonderful that somebody had the foresight to build a course surrounded by such beauty. It's like that movie *Field of Dreams*: build it and they will come. And they are still coming, because it's sheer perfection.

MARGUERITE PENROSE

THE CASINO AT MARINO

MARGUERITE PENROSE was born in a Dublin mother-and-baby home in 1974, the daughter of an Irish mother and a Zambian father. Adopted into a loving family, she grew up living with scoliosis and having to navigate the world as an active woman of colour with a disability. Today she is an activist and writer, contributing articles to the *Irish Independent* and *The Journal*, and the bestselling author of her memoir, *Yeah, But Where Are You Really From?*

Three miles from Dublin city centre, the eighteenth-century Casino at Marino was built as a fifty-foot square pleasure house for James Caulfeild, the first Earl of Charlemont. Casino means "little house" but the name is deceptive and this is a place where nothing is quite as it seems. Inside this seemingly miniature architectural gem there are sixteen rooms, including service rooms, a library, reception rooms and bedrooms on the upper floor. When Marguerite Penrose first saw it she was mesmerised, as so many visitors are . . .

In fifth year, I must have been around seventeen, I was taken to the Casino at Marino for a school trip. I went to Santa Sabina school in Sutton, which is not too far from the Casino. I did art in school. I was no good, not like my sister, who was really talented, but I loved being creative. I got really into art history for the Leaving Cert. We were taken all over the city to see different types of architecture; I fell in love with Georgian Dublin and buildings like James Gandon's Custom House. At the time I had a wonderful art teacher, Naomi Cassidy; she was one of those cool teachers. Everybody loved her classes. She knew I wasn't the best artist but she never gave up on me. She could see I flourished in the art history side of things.

The first thing I remember noticing when we went up to the Casino was that it looked tiny from the outside. That's the

"I was fascinated about how it went from an idea in someone's head to a drawing on paper to this astonishing building."

"I remember looking at the walls and the details; it felt like something you'd see in Rome."

magic of the place. Then when you go inside you realise it is much bigger, a bit like *Dr Who's* Tardis. It has sixteen rooms but you'd never guess that when you are standing outside. I remember walking around just being so delighted by all the optical illusions that were woven into the architecture. There are these massive columns and they are hollow because they are hiding all the guttering and pipes inside. You can't see through the windows because of how the glass is designed. And that's deliberate, so when looking from the outside it's impossible to know exactly how it's laid out inside. From the exterior it looks like it is a one-storey building, but it's actually three floors. On the roof, you see these decorative urns but they are really chimney tops. That is achieved with a lot of architectural tricks: for example, the doors and windows somehow appear much smaller than they actually are.

I just remember thinking it was such a clever design and I was fascinated about how it went from an idea in someone's head to a drawing on paper, to this astonishing building. It was designed for James Caulfeild by Sir William Chambers. The build began in 1750 and it wasn't finished until 1775, so it took a bit of time to complete. It's neo-classical. I remember looking at the walls and the details; it felt like something you'd see in Rome, and apparently it's one of the finest buildings of its style in Europe outside of Italy. I remember it was cold going around the Casino; I think that was something to do with the stone. I was particularly struck by the Zodiac room, which has a dome with all the astrological symbols. Being into astrology myself, I love that in 1750 people were thinking star signs should be incorporated into a building of such splendour.

I know nobody actually lived in it, the Casino was just a folly for Caulfeild and his posh friends, but when I was there I found myself thinking, what if I lived here back in that time? What kind of clothes would I have worn, how would I have spent my days? It fired my imagination and I don't think I've ever been so blown

away by a building ever in Ireland. It makes me so proud that it's in Dublin.

Looking back, half of the people on the school tour didn't really seem to care about the building. They just wanted to go back to school and paint something. But I wanted the fantastic tour guides to tell me more. I don't think anybody could visit without something being stirred up in them. Everybody should visit the Casino at least once. You could not fail to be impressed by this perfect place.

CHRIS DE BURGH

DALKEY VILLAGE

CHRIS DE BURGH is an incredibly successful singer-songwriter who has sold over 45 million albums worldwide and is known for hits such as "Lady in Red" which achieved no. 1 status in forty-seven countries and the Christmas classic, "A Spaceman Came Travelling". De Burgh continues to make music, releasing his twenty-seventh studio album, *The Legend of Robin Hood*, in 2021, alongside his other interests as an avid historian and wine collector.

Dalkey is a postcard-pretty village by the sea in south Co. Dublin. The village is popular with tourists and home to the annual Dalkey Book Festival which attracts hundreds of bibliophiles each summer. Actor Matt Damon was spotted there during the pandemic when he was staying with U2's Bono, who lives nearby. The area is also associated with writers such as Maeve Binchy and George Bernard Shaw. For Chris de Burgh, who bought a house there in the 1980s, Dalkey is a place that has everything he needs . . .

When Diane and I got married we started off in a small apartment in Seapoint, but by the time our daughter Rosanna was two years old we felt it was time to move on. A friend of ours said we should go and look at this house on Rockfort Avenue in Dalkey Village. A man had inherited the house from his two eccentric aunts, the Tyson sisters. They drove a Rolls Royce and went around on motorbikes in the 1900s. They were very unusual ladies, way ahead of their time.

The house had been built by one of their ancestors, possibly their grandfather, and used as a holiday home for rich folk coming to the village from Dublin. I struck a deal with the man who owned it which included a piece of land that butts onto Sorrento Road. That bit of land is now used as a secret garden by the Dalkey Book Festival for their wonderful event each summer.

We bought the house in 1985 but we did a fair bit of construction, so Rosanna would have been three by the time we actually moved in. Then our two boys came along, Hubie in 1988 and Michael in 1990. The house was perfect for children. We had this large, south-facing garden with high walls so it was very safe and they could play and explore all day. What was marvellous was that we could enjoy the peace and solitude in this beautiful, quiet garden and then in ninety seconds we could be out the back gate right in the thick of the village atmosphere of Dalkey.

I'd had a music career for over a decade by then, but in 1986, the year we moved into the house, my song "Lady in Red" was released and became a big hit all over the world. I was a little bit more reclusive at this point in my life. The song was number one in the UK and I wasn't that keen on walking down the main street of Dalkey having people singing the song at me. I also got a bit sick of guys standing beside me at the urinal in the pub singing drunken versions of "Lady in Red".

Around that more reclusive time I created a sort of pub in my house. I bought a keg of Smithwicks and a big chiller and lots of pint glasses and installed them in my wine cellar. That was a time in my career when I would have been doing a twelve-night run of concerts in the RDS. The band would come back to my house after the gigs and we'd have parties. They were brilliant times.

DUCKHORN
DUCKHORN
DUCKHORN
FRANCE
MIND THE STEP
BAROLO

"Going to The Grapevine is like visiting the library for me – I enjoy reading the labels on the bottles."

Eventually we moved to Bushey Park in Enniskerry, Co. Wicklow, a place we spent seven years renovating. We never sold the Dalkey house. I didn't like the idea of the kids driving past one day saying, "That's where we used to live." I wanted them to still be able to go there. So we kept the house and had various tenants over the years.

The children are grown up now and have moved out, so it's a good time to move back to Dalkey. We've been doing up the house over the last few years, making it even more comfortable for us and for the grandchildren when they come to stay. I'm looking forward to moving back in. I'm conscious of getting older. When I'm in my dotage I want to be able to walk out of my door and straight into the village.

"The main street of Dalkey has a sort of Mediterranean vibe . . . On weekends the place is jammed and loads of fun."

Everything I need is there. The DART of course, which is so handy, and the last time I checked I think I counted seventeen pubs and restaurants in the village. I'm a wine collector, so I spend a lot of time in The Grapevine, the local wine shop that's run by a charming couple. Going to The Grapevine is like visiting the library for me – I enjoy reading the labels on the bottles.

Across the road is the 1909 restaurant. That's where I often meet the "Pauls" for our marathon lunches. The Pauls are a group of friends of mine, all called Paul. I bring my own wines to our lunches and we'll have a laugh tasting them all. It's rather embarrassing because our lunches tend to go on so long that sometimes we are still there when the dinner service begins.

We couldn't meet during lockdown, so during the pandemic I started a wine club on Zoom with the Pauls. They say women are good talkers but we are the champions of chatter. I think our longest talking-and-wine-drinking Zoom session was over five hours.

Since it's been done up, the main street of Dalkey has a sort of Mediterranean vibe. We've got tables outside several restaurants such as Ouzo's and De Ville's and there are a couple of gorgeous delicatessens, not forgetting a fantastic SuperValu made famous by Matt Damon who was photographed carrying one of their plastic shopping bags.

Dalkey has a really active community council. They've helped make the village a real mecca for tourists especially during the summer months. On weekends the place is jammed and loads of fun.

I've always had a deep respect for and interest in history. The village has been so well maintained and preserved over the years which means that when you are walking through Dalkey you are looking at a very similar view to one people would have experienced a hundred years ago.

The previous owner of my house in Dalkey left a load of old photographs behind. His ancestors used to play tennis on the back lawn and in one of the photos there were people in the garden with rackets and two little girls sitting in a pram. Those little girls were the Tyson sisters, who went on to live and die in the house. The picture moved me very much and years ago I wrote a song about it called "Shine On":

I was looking at a photograph,
Taken in a garden long before the war . . .
We've got to learn,
We must leave here a garden for our
children,
When we are gone forever

It's a song about everything we leave behind. I like the idea of leaving something for those who come after us. I want my grandchildren to play in that garden. To see them there, in the place where my own children used to run when they were small, is quite a thrill. I feel the same delight about Dalkey Village – it should be protected and maintained for future generations to enjoy.

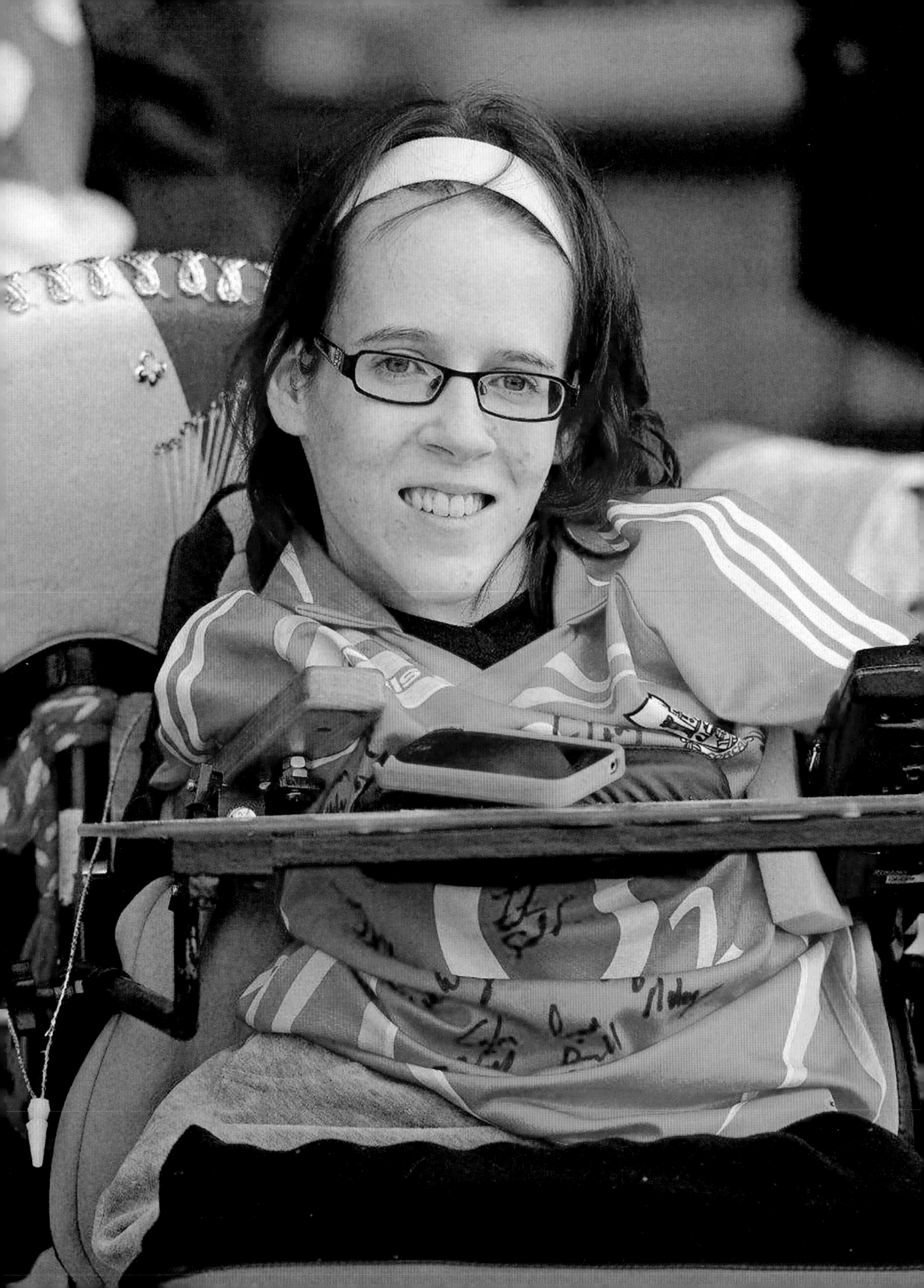

JOANNE O'RIORDAN
GAELIC GROUNDS, LIMERICK

JOANNE O'RIORDAN is a journalist, activist and podcaster from Co. Cork. Born with the condition Tetra-amelia, she reversed the Irish government's decision to cut disability payments in 2011. She has since had a film based on her life, *No Limbs No Limits*, appeared on *The Late Late Show* in Ireland, addressed the United Nations (receiving a standing ovation) and was named Young Person of the Year twice amongst many other awards and achievements. O' Riordan currently writes a sports column every Thursday for *The Irish Times*.

Gaelic Grounds or Páirc na nGael, as it is known as Gaeilge, is the main GAA stadium in Limerick city. The grounds are home to both the Limerick hurling and football teams. With a capacity of nearly 50,000, it has seen major sporting clashes since it was first set up in 1928. Though she is a proud Cork woman, it's a place that feels like a home from home for Joanne O'Riordan . . .

I was born with a rare disability known as Tetra-amelia; in other words, I was born without limbs. This hasn't stopped me pursuing a career as a sports journalist and being a disability activist. That's not to say I haven't had setbacks. In 2012 I had to have a very serious twelve-hour back operation. They put a titanium rod in my back to help with my scoliosis, so that the curvature of my spine wouldn't get any worse.

As I often do, I set myself a little marker for something to achieve after the surgery. I wanted to get to the Gaelic Grounds in Limerick. Cork were playing Limerick in the Munster Senior football final and whether Cork won or lost I wanted to be there.

It was important for me to get back into the normal run of life. Weekends are match days for me. They suggest routine

and normality. So that was the goal, to get back to my regular routine. I was in hospital for five days. I was desperate to get out and get to the game.

Unfortunately, there was an issue with the stitches. My skin knitted back together too well and I had to be rushed back to the hospital to get my stitches out.

Even through all of that I was saying, "I'm getting to the game, I'm getting to the game" and meanwhile my dad was saying, "Joanne, the game is going to kill you."

My dad has a childhood friend who was a Cork selector at the time; he and the football team would have been constantly in touch while I was in hospital. They sent me up a card, signed by all the players, and a jersey. So, when match day came around, I was determined to get to the Gaelic Grounds and that's what I did. I was just like a regular fan that day, which is what I wanted, but I look back at pictures of myself at the stadium now and my colour is not good. How someone let me out, I don't know. I was so happy to be there, to have that sense of normality and hang out with my dad just soaking up the atmosphere.

"I was so happy to be at the game, to have that sense of normality and hang out with my dad, just soaking up the atmosphere."

I was being very careful with my back obviously, but I was so thrilled to be at the game. A man came over to me, part of the Sombrero Gang in Cork GAA. He gave me his sombrero for the day. My neck was mangled with screws and titanium holding it up, so I could not wear a sombrero but I wanted to be part of the game, just be like everyone else, a regular fan. I put on that sombrero out of sheer determination.

I have such a beautiful memory of that day despite the pain I was in.

In most sports stadiums the wheelchair section is pushed to the back usually out to the side. It's not like that in the Gaelic Grounds. They are up front and centre, right next to the subs benches, and you feel much more part of the game. You are not shoved in a corner and forgotten about, you get to feel the atmosphere and be in with the crowd. So many people were coming over to me all the time, wishing me well, being so kind. And I'd never experienced that.

I then got the delight of my sixteen-year-old life. Cork won and my favourite player at that time, Eoin Cadogan, came over and presented me with his match-day jersey. Even though I hadn't washed in around two weeks because of the operation, I remember telling my dad, "I'm not washing this jersey either." Afterwards, the team invited me to their dinner and told me that my back operation and everything I was going through had inspired their win.

When I go there, it reminds me of that brilliant day and how connected I felt to everybody. Other people might not agree, they might think there are better grounds, better facilities, and perhaps that's true. All I know is that it's very rare as a wheelchair user to feel part of the crowd and part of the experience the way I do at the Gaelic Grounds. When I'm there I have a constant smile on my face. It doesn't matter if you have a disability, you can hang around and be with everyone. You are not excluded. That's what makes it perfect.

ARDAL O'HANLON
HERBERT PARK, DUBLIN

ARDAL O'HANLON is one of Ireland's best loved actors and comedians. From Carrickmacross in Co. Monaghan, and known for his roles in *Father Ted*, *Death in Paradise* and *Derry Girls*, he tours his stand-up comedy worldwide and has appeared on panel shows such as *Taskmaster* and *Would I Lie To You*. Ardal has made numerous documentary films and his second novel, *Brouhaha* was described by the Irish Times as, "an Irish literary classic if it wasn't so damned funny".

Herbert Park, located in the heart of the Dublin suburb of Ballsbridge, was once part of the vast Fitzwilliam estate. In the early 1900s it was given over to the local council for public use. It's a bustling suburban park with tennis, boules and croquet courts, a bowling green, soccer pitches and children's playgrounds. For a time during the 1980s, Ardal O'Hanlon spent a significant amount of time there and it's his nostalgia for this period that makes Herbert Park his perfect place . . .

As parks go, Herbert Park is perfectly pleasant, although I should point out that I'm not a connoisseur of municipal parks by any means. I chose it more for what the park represents to me: a time in my life from around 1981 to 1991 when I was relatively carefree and had no idea what I wanted to do with my life.

My first encounter with the park was celebrating the results of my Inter Cert exams, known as the Junior Cert now. I was at boarding school at Blackrock College but we got the night off for the occasion. We found a quiet corner of the park to drink in, celebrating this very Irish rite of passage where everyone turns a blind eye to teenagers getting wasted. I would have been fourteen and had around three cans of beer probably, the most I'd ever drunk up to that point. It was a great park like that, easy enough to gain access and more importantly easy to get out of later on, even when it was closed. My sister was at college and lived close by, so we chose the park because we knew we'd have somewhere to crash later on.

After I left school I went to college and ended up in this dingy bedsit near

"I just went there to dream and muse and read and kick a ball."

"It felt like Herbert Park was my garden, a refuge from the hassles of the city."

Herbert Park. In those days, even in the most salubrious suburbs of Dublin like Donnybrook and Ballsbridge there were still some houses that were divided into decrepit flats full of writers, musicians and poets. Dublin was a bit more bohemian then. I lived near the park for around seven or eight years. I wouldn't say they were the happiest days of my life but they were easy and free. I had no expectations, no responsibilities, no children, no mortgage and no audience. Nobody knew who I was. It felt like Herbert Park was my garden, a refuge from the hassles of the city.

I played football there every day of my life in those years. It wasn't organised. We'd no mobile phones. There was no way of contacting people and you didn't even know the names of the people you were playing with. You just rocked up to the park at around six or seven in the evening, particularly in the summer months, and just joined a game. Maybe I'm idealising it a bit, but it felt like a lovely time. I had my head in the clouds. I was putting off any big life decisions and sort of convinced myself I could put them off forever.

When I wasn't playing football you'd have found me sitting on a bench on my own in the park reading pretentious William Somerset Maugham novels, or *Portrait of the Artist As a Young Man*. I pretty much knew every duck in the park by name. I had no idea what I wanted to do with my life, so I just went there to dream and muse and read and kick a ball. I look back on that time very fondly, even though it was a time when I had no prospects and no income. I was also beginning to dabble in comedy at the time and the two people I started out with were Barry Murphy and Kevin Gildea. We'd meet in my bedsit quite a lot and pretend to write sketches for hours. And then at one point, you'd see people's legs begin to drum up and down and that was the signal to go to the park for football.

Later in life, when I couldn't play football anymore – too many injuries – I got into tennis. Now I think of it, Herbert Park was the first place I ever played that sport. There was a guy in the park who was in charge of the courts, he had one of those leather bus conductor satchels and he'd give you a ticket for the tennis. His little joke when he gave you your ticket was "seats upstairs".

When we made the decision to move back from London and raise our kids in Dublin

we ended up living not too far from Herbert Park. I've stood there on the sidelines on Sundays while my own son played with his football club. It was a place I was drawn to in those lockdown days when we were all walking around like zombies. Walking the dog, I'd take one turn and the next and somehow, without thinking, end up in the park. I felt comfortable there and very safe. I learned a lot about the park at that time. I looked at every tree, every plaque. That's how I know that in 1907, the park hosted the famous Dublin International Trades Exhibition with exhibits from across the British Empire, including an entire Somalian village and a Canadian water chute. The duck pond was actually built to house the water chute. Sadly, any traces of that exhibition are now long gone.

I've travelled widely in my life and there are lots of perfect places in Ireland and the rest of the world but I keep finding myself back in the park. There's just such an aura of calm – I mean people are playing lawn bowls there for God's sake. I've never played it myself and I probably never will, but it's a timeless, civilised and genteel pursuit. It's a balm for the soul just watching people play that game. And Herbert Park has been a balm in my life too.

MARIAN KEYES
LAHINCH, CO. CLARE

MARIAN KEYES is the multi-million-copy, bestselling author of some of the most widely loved novels of the past thirty years. *Again Rachel*, the sequel to the groundbreaking *Rachel's Holiday*, was Marian's fifteenth novel. Others include *This Charming Man*, *Anybody Out There* and *Grownups*. Marian uses her position to raise awareness of some of the most challenging issues of our time, including addiction, immigration, depression, domestic violence and abortion rights.

Lahinch is a seaside town at the head of Liscannor Bay, Co. Clare. Generations of Irish families have flocked to this 2km stretch of sand for traditional bucket and spade holidays. More recently, the soaring waves attract surfers and canoeists from all over the world. In Percy French's song, "Are Ye Right There Michael?" the town was commemorated for its beauty: "At Lahinch the sea shines like a jewel, with joy you are ready to shout." It certainly makes Marian Keyes shout for joy . . .

There is only one sea, in my opinion. That's the Atlantic, which is the best ocean, the very best sea. There is no debate. It's a proper sea: powerful and unpredictable, wild and impressive. No other sea comes close. I know people speak highly of the Indian Ocean and people are, I believe, very fond of the Mediterranean. They are all grand in their ways but they are not the Irish Atlantic, as seen from Lahinch. The very best sea.

Clearly, I "drank the kool-aid" at a very young age. I have such happy childhood memories of Lahinch. I remember going down to the rock pools with our fluorescent green and pink nets and spending hours down there on the strand. I have photos of me and my siblings building sandcastles on the beach. My mum went there as a child, because she lived nearby, and my dad loved it because he grew up in Limerick city. He spent hours walking the sand dunes, which you can't do any more since the golf club went up, but I remember when we could walk them for miles. And you can still walk the beach almost to Liscannor.

"When I first got together with my husband Tony, I had to bring him to Lahinch to find out if he loved it as much as I did. If he didn't love Lahinch I knew there'd be trouble ahead. But of course, he did."

I've written about Lahinch in two books – *This Charming Man* and *The Last Chance Saloon*. I mean, how could I not? It's fabulous. I bought a house there, which all my family and our friends use. The house is right on the sea, and on the first floor of the house you can't see the ground because we're so close to the water. It feels a lot like being on a ship. I can just sit there for hours watching the waves coming and going, the tides drifting in and out. It's just so calming and soothing.

I take great delight in the fact that my mother went to Lahinch as a child, I went there as a child and now the next generation of my family go there, the smaller ones and the bigger ones. My nephew Luka, who is twenty-one, was just in Lahinch with his girlfriend and it means so much to me that this is a place everyone still wants to visit. I do think even if I hadn't been introduced to the town at such a young age, I would still think it's just the most wondrous place. I learned to swim in that sea. It is never boring and always magnificent. Sometimes the waves are crashing in and other days it's just layer after layer of very genteel waves. Some days there will be loads of rocks thrown up; on others the sea will spit up crowds of jellyfish or seaweed.

What I really love is arriving down to Lahinch on that first day. You can't even push open the car door sometimes with the wind. And then it hits you, that blast of sea air and the salty smell. I am instantly catapulted back to childhood, to when I was five or eight or fifteen.

I always meet people I know or am related to; another great thing about the town for me. The townspeople of Lahinch are both gas and lovely. When I first got together with my husband Tony, I had to bring him to Lahinch to find out if he loved it as much as I did. If he didn't love Lahinch I knew there'd be trouble ahead. But of course, he did.

In the interest of full transparency, I should mention that Lahinch used to be a "falling down" kind of town. It's come on quite a bit, there is a lot of sourdough about the place, even a food truck and of course the very cool surfing community. In the last twenty-five years, it's become this deeply surfy place. So there are all the young fellas and women driving around

with surfboards on their roof racks and everywhere you look there's a wetsuit hanging out to dry.

But even with all the changes I find people stick to the same rituals: the 99s, the pots of tea, the bracing walks, the fish and chips. The pubs in Lahinch do tend to divide people, which can be awkward when you are going for your toasted sandwich. I mean are you a Kenny's person or a Shamrock Inn person? I'm a Shamrock person. I like that the soup of the day there is always mushroom and the cheesecake of the day is always strawberry.

I'll usually take my toasted sandwich in the Shamrock during the summer but I have it in the Corner Stone Bar in the winter when the town empties out and becomes a very different, quieter place. I love Lahinch even more in the winter. When there is terrible weather in Ireland, like the big storms that end up on the news, they always show that bit of the promenade where my house is, to demonstrate the awful conditions. One year the storm was so bad our windows were all smashed in by the wind and the waves but we have them well protected now with shutters.

When I got into oil painting there for a while, all I was interested in painting were massive Lahinch seascapes, the glorious moodiness of the Atlantic Ocean. The best sea. Constant and ever-changing. The sounds and the smells. The colours. Dark grey or navy or sparkling blueish green depending on the time of day or year. I've images imprinted in my mind of storms coming from miles across the water, those silver needles of rain falling in the distance, the light changing and the clouds shifting. You can feel the energy of the ocean, bigger and more powerful than anything us humans can muster. In conclusion, if you haven't been yet I implore you to go and experience the majesty of Lahinch for yourself. Order a toastie at the Shamrock and tell them Marian sent you.

“My mother went to Lahinch as a child, I went there as a child and now the next generation of my family go there.”

SENATOR LYNN RUANE

THE MOUNTAINS, TALLAGHT

SENATOR LYNN RUANE grew up in Tallaght and gained national attention representing student parents on the Trinity College Dublin Students' Union executive. Lynn was elected the union's president in 2015, leading her to represent Trinity graduates in the 25th Seanad Éireann. She was re-elected in 2020 for her commitment to social justice, equality and equitable access to education. Lynn was vice-chair of the special Joint Oireachtas Committee on the Eighth Amendment and was named Senator of the Year in 2016 by *The Irish Times*. Her autobiography *People Like Me* was released in 2018 and she has since graduated from Dublin City University with a master's in Creative Writing.

Tallaght is a large satellite town in south Co. Dublin, a sprawling suburb developed in the 1970s. In addition to the busy retail centre The Square, the area is part of the Dublin Mountains Way which is accessed by Sean Walsh Park. Lynn Ruane is a proud Tallaght woman who has recently discovered even more to admire about her area . . .

I live in Killinarden in Tallaght. I grew up here, in the foothills of the Dublin Mountains. The crazy thing is that as a kid, it somehow didn't feel like we were at the slopes of mountains. We were deeply urban children living so close to the countryside and yet we were so disconnected from it, as though some invisible force field was keeping us away from the vast natural resource on our doorstep. Over the last ten years I've begun to see the mountains differently. I've been asking why all that natural magnificence felt so distant from us growing up. And wondering how we might get close to the mountains again.

As teenagers, if I'm honest, the only time we went up to the mountains was during mushroom season. Or sometimes we'd wander farmers' fields and they'd let their

"It was like we ignored the magic of the mountains all this time and now we're recognising it as part of us, as part of Tallaght."

guns off and we'd run. We didn't know our way around the mountains we lived beside. It's why we strayed into farmers' property. We didn't know the paths and the routes that would take us where we needed to go.

When I first started thinking about it a few years ago, I felt a loss for Tallaght and the fact that nobody had engaged us with the land. When I was growing up we were always given out to for being on horses and these days it's the same thing with the kids on their scrambler bikes. And all the while there is this vast resource, a place that could be utilised to create youth spaces with kids on horses or riding bikes in a state-of-the-art scrambler park and be given the chance to really get to know this incredible local landscape.

In the last couple of years they've built a pathway from the residential area of Ellensborough into the mountains. It feels like the first time that we've looked out from the back of the estates and something has been inviting us in. It feels like the beginning of an acknowledgement that we should have access to the mountains. I'm excited by the idea that the pathway is an invitation to Tallaght residents to start exploring a resource we've been separated from for so long.

The new walkway goes past the nursing home where my dad spent the last months of his life. Before the pathway was created, I used to put him in a wheelchair and wheel him up to the reservoir at Bohernabreena. Now, with the pathway, you see people jogging up there, walking with their dogs and their kids. People are painting rocks and putting them under trees to remember friends and relatives they've lost.

I brought the photographer up to this particular hill in Kiltipper for a reason. First because it's got the most amazing view, even though we're only up a very small hill. When you look back you can see Tallaght and the pyramid of The Square shopping centre. When you look ahead you can see the hills and the countryside. But it's also that point between you venturing off into the mountains and leaving Tallaght behind. A sort of call to adventure. You can also see Dublin Bay from up there, and if you turn slightly to the right you can see Poolbeg Towers.

When I was young, getting to the seaside from Tallaght was an ordeal: a bus into town then another bus or a DART out to a seaside spot. It could be a few hours before you'd get near the sea, it felt so far

“I’m excited by the idea that the pathway is an invitation to Tallaght residents to start exploring.”

away. I never felt like I was from anywhere except Tallaght. But all that time, we had a view of the whole of Dublin and if we'd have seen that, really known that, it might have expanded our minds a little in the 1980s. We would have had the mountains and the sea spread out in front of us, and that's something we missed as kids.

I go exploring up there now. I take paths not knowing where they might lead and challenge myself to find my way back down the mountain again. One time when I was up there, I heard a birdcall and I knew it was a woodpecker. That is not something that is associated with Tallaght. When people think of Tallaght they tend to think of violence, drugs and crime; the outside perceptions of the place can be so narrow when actually Tallaght is much more than that. It's a place where I can hear a woodpecker just a fifteen-minute walk from my house. A place where you can follow the Dodder River from Tallaght all the way into the city.

My school was at the foot of the mountains. Why didn't we spend more time up there? Why weren't we taught about the flora and the fauna and the trees and the woodpeckers and all the rest of the wildlife? We could have learned hiking and survival skills. Our connection to our surroundings would have been much deeper instead of only feeling connected to our concrete estates. It was like we ignored the magic of the mountains all this time and now we're recognising it as part of us, as part of Tallaght.

It might sound strange but I truly didn't see the mountains properly when I was a kid growing up. Now, I look out my bedroom window, and it's as though I'm seeing them for the first time. That invisible forcefield that once separated us is gone. Now, I take the time to gaze out the window feeling grateful that hopefully I have another few decades left to properly explore the mountains just outside my back door.

KEVIN SHARKEY

SHARKEY GALLERY

KEVIN SHARKEY is one of Ireland's most successful artists. During a very difficult childhood, he discovered many talents, including painting, dancing and songwriting. After an Irish dancing career, he became the first mixed-race presenter on Irish TV and had appearances on *Father Ted*. He has sold over 10,000 paintings worldwide and has three galleries in Dublin, London and Barcelona with artwork collected by celebrities and presidents alongside being admitted to the Mel T Sutcliffe collection, which includes the world's top artists.

The Sharkey Gallery is on the Royal Hibernian Way on Dawson Street. It is a showcase for Kevin Sharkey's work, colourful, contemporary abstracts, which range in price from €5,000 to over €100,000 and can also be viewed in his online gallery. Sharkey began painting at the age of twelve but only started showing his work in his late thirties. Established in 2021, he says the sweetly smelling exhibition space is his perfect place . . .

I've been an artist all of my life, but a public artist for the last twenty-five years. Art was always an escape for me. It was a cure for loneliness. I was twelve and a half years old when I did my first painting. I had been adopted from a mother and baby home by a Donegal family when I was six months old. My experiences with them were horrific and violent. I was the only Black kid in the county and it wasn't easy. When I was twelve years old my adopted parents changed their mind and sent me back to the orphanage, which was the worst thing I've ever had to deal with. I cried all the time.

One day a woman came in with a box of paints and said she thought they might cheer me up. So I painted a little painting for the next twenty minutes and I remember that as a light bulb moment. I realised I wasn't lonely for the twenty minutes while I was painting. I wasn't sad. All my life painting has been an escape and a safe haven. It's become incredibly healing. No matter where you are in your own head, however dark it seems, you can take one step towards the light by making something beautiful.

"However dark it seems, you can take one step towards the light by making something beautiful."

"I had to take some huge risks and they didn't always work out. But the man who made no mistakes made nothing."

Whenever I felt down, and there have been some very hard times in my life, I would cook, or I would paint or make music. I've been a head chef, I've written music for bands and I've always made art. If you spend your life creating things for people and bringing beauty into the world, you are on the right frequency – that's what I think anyway. I see the ripples of gratification. When people come in and respond to my work it gives me great joy.

There is no point in learning to make beautiful things, whether it's food or music or art, unless you are sharing all of those things with people. That's what makes it even more pleasurable. Five months ago I set up the Sharkey Gallery in Dublin. It really is my perfect place.

When I am in the gallery, I am surrounded by art that I created. Being a self-taught artist, it is a wonderful luxury to be able to look around a gallery full of your work and say, "I created this world." I chose the colour of the paint on the walls, I chose the lighting, I chose the fresh flowers. I don't take it for granted. Being an artist is a very lonely pursuit – you can't do it in the pub, it's not a social activity – the reward is seeing people in the gallery. I am obviously in the business of selling my paintings but looking at them is free. Even if they are not buying, the very fact that people are connecting with something I created that is hanging in this beautiful environment is so rewarding. Seeing people's reactions is beautiful.

It's almost a sacred space to me, the gallery. I grew up being dragged off to Mass every Sunday whether you wanted to go or not. I dealt with the boredom by looking at the stained-glass windows. We're talking about Donegal in the 1960s: the church was a grim building with no colour, except for the windows which would come alive when the light hit them. It took me years to realise that was my first interaction with colour. That colour relationship plays a huge part in how I create my paintings. They are bold and colourful and in your face.

I've never had a penny from the Arts Council or had even a canvas given to me. I've done what I've done through hard work and talent. I'm proud of myself because nobody helped me do this. I had to take some huge risks and they didn't always work out. But the man who made no mistakes made nothing.

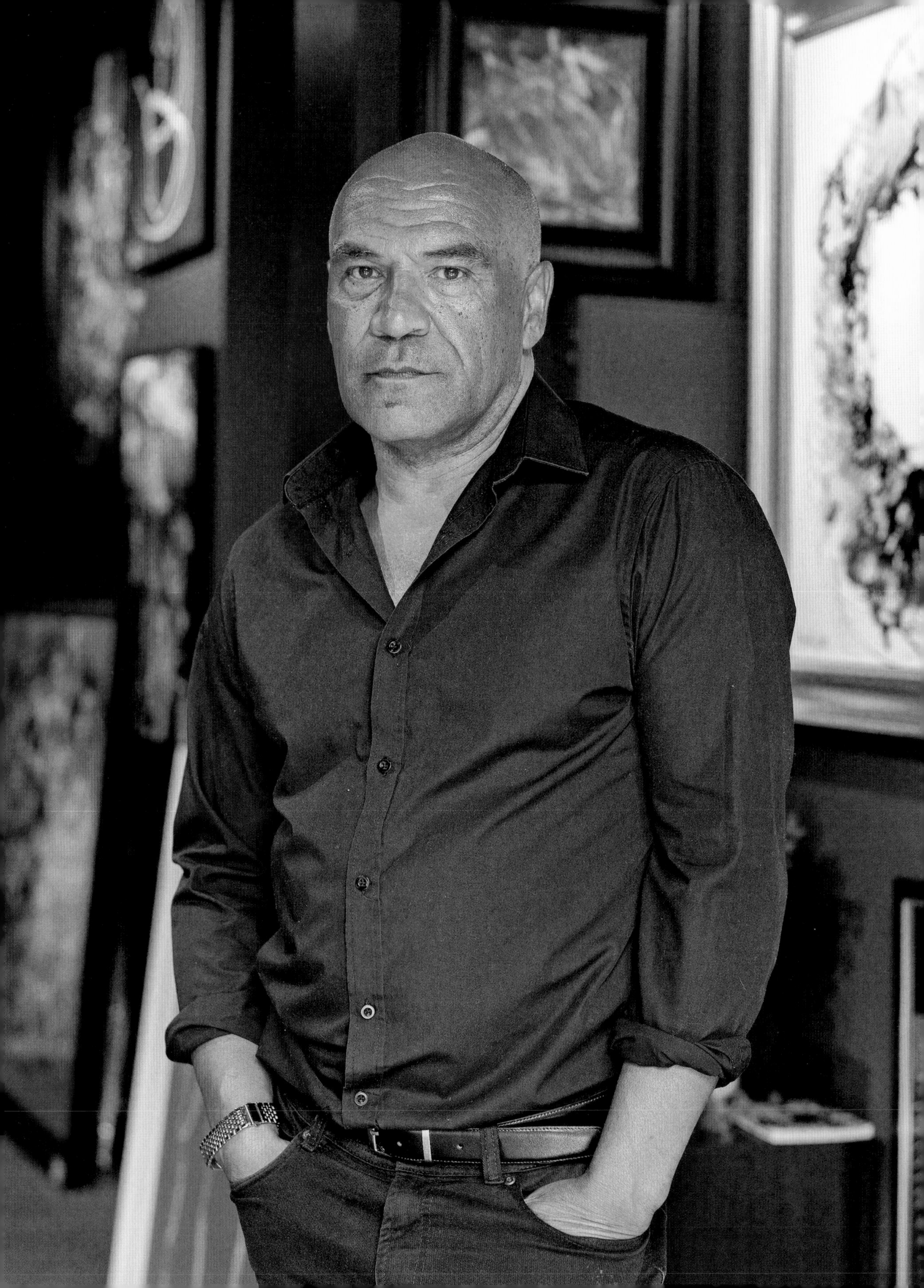

In the gallery, it's like I'm playing house. As someone said to me one day, "That's a lovely smell, what is it?" And I told them, "That's the smell of money."

The candles I burn there cost €80 each. There's an assault on your senses as soon as you come in, setting the tone before you even get a chance to see the art. I make sure there is music playing in the background because people want to have conversations, but they don't always want you to hear. The music disguises their conversation, especially if they are saying something like, "Jesus, they're expensive, let's get out of here."

The gallery is a place for browsing and for appreciating the work. The sales are a huge bonus. For the past few years my work has been bought by a collector of Picasso and Francis Bacon. When I passed the 10,000 paintings sold mark, I thought to myself "you're good at this". But I've had to learn how to be a shopkeeper, that is something not all artists understand. There are a lot of talented artists out there but they can't accept that what they create is a product. It needs to be in a shop. That's the one thing they don't teach kids in art school. You need to bring the work to the customers. If you don't accept that you are a manufacturer of products then you are going to have a very miserable existence as an artist. I've learned how to live as an artist and as a shopkeeper. Now the gallery is like a church to me and I'm the happiest man you'll ever meet.

MICHELLE FAIRLEY
RATHLIN ISLAND

MICHELLE FAIRLEY is an actor from Coleraine known for playing Catelyn Stark in the HBO series *Game of Thrones* and Mrs Granger in the *Harry Potter and the Deathly Hallows* films. She also has recurring roles on many popular television programmes including *Suits*, *24: Live Another Day* and *Gangs of London*. Michelle is also an accomplished theatre actress, winning a Clarence Derwent Award for her role in *Julius Caesar* to accompany her Best Actress Irish Film & Television Award for *Game of Thrones*.

Six miles long and one mile wide, Rathlin Island is off the Co. Antrim coast at Ballycastle, and has a population of around 140. The rugged, L-shaped island is teeming with wildlife and is home to tens of thousands of seabirds including puffins, kittiwakes and razorbills, making it a popular spot for birdwatchers. It's in Rathlin's caves that Robert the Bruce is said to have encountered the spider which inspired him to not give up the fight for Scottish independence. For Michelle Fairley, Rathlin represents friendship and a tranquil, perfect place of reflection . . .

My perfect place is a spot with a panoramic view in my brilliant friend Jacqueline's garden on Rathlin Island. It's the garden of the home that she and some of her siblings built on Rathlin. Her uncle sold them a piece of land, and they built this house on an elevated site there around ten years ago.

Jacqui and I grew up and went to school together in Ballycastle and she has a strong family connection to Rathlin Island – her mother was born there and her father was a lighthouse keeper, back when they still had manual lighthouses.

The view is simply astonishing. We sit there chatting at the front of the house, which on good days gets drenched in sun all afternoon. There is so much geography laid out in front of you, it's hard to know where to look. If you turn your head to the left, you've got Scotland: twenty-nine kilometres away you can clearly see the Mull of Kintyre. If you look straight ahead you are looking onto Fair Head mountain cliff on the northeastern coast of Co. Antrim on the mainland. Then you can see the golf course behind it, right up to the mountains around Ballycastle. If you keep looking along down the coast you can eventually see the Giant's Causeway and even Donegal.

I grew up looking over at Rathlin from Ballycastle, the other view. Back then it was a lot harder to get onto the island because there were no ferries and you had to rely on a fisherman's boat. Of course, if the weather was bad they wouldn't go. So it was a lot more perilous. If anybody was ill, it was a helicopter job to get them off. Now there are ferries, a fast one or a slow one, there's not really much difference between them.

I love sitting there with Jacqui just chatting and telling stories. I'm based in London, so when I think of Rathlin and that view, it reminds me of her and of the places of our childhood. So many memories of the beach and the golf course and swimming in the sea and walking horses on the strand. It's like the place that made me is stretched out in front of us, every landmark of our lives visible from the front of her house. When I'm on Rathlin, looking out over that extraordinary view, it feels like I am able to look at my life, my formative years, from a fresh perspective.

I was there recently, in glorious weather. The sun bouncing off the water, so calm and tranquil. The house overlooks the harbour, so you can see all the activity with the boats, people coming in and out of the pub.

It tests my nerves, Rathlin. I get really bad seasickness. To go around the island in a boat I am just waiting to be sick. But I am always amazed that I don't. I adore the wildness of the place and the fact that it's still so sparsely populated. If you want to be alone, you can be, but there is also enough activity to stop you getting bored. On a Saturday evening, you might see all the boats arriving, the people walking onto the harbour heading for the pub. Everybody is happy to arrive on the island, people go there knowing they will be able to relax.

We don't always have to speak when we're looking out at that view. There's no need for words. I just love being able to

"It's like the place that made me is stretched out in front of us, every landmark of our lives visible from the front of her house."

"There is so much geography
laid out in front of you, it's hard to
know where to look."

sit on another landmass and see Ireland. I did that from the other side, many years ago when I was in Scotland one summer filming. We had a night off and we went to the Mull of Kintyre and from there I could see Fair Head and Rathlin and I found it incredibly emotional. I burst into tears.

I am glad *Game of Thrones* has given people something else to talk about in terms of Northern Ireland – our stunningly beautiful scenery. And so many people are returning there from places around the world, bringing back what they've learned to Northern Ireland, making it a more international and tolerant place to live.

MAÏA DUNPHY
DALKEY QUARRY

MAÏA DUNPHY is an Irish television producer, broadcaster and writer. Raised in Dalkey, she graduated from Trinity College Dublin and has written regularly for *The Irish Times*, the *Irish Independent Insider Magazine* and the *Evening Herald* among others. She has written her own book, *The M Word*, and produced many comedy shows and three documentary series of her own, whilst appearing on *Dancing With the Stars* and *Celebrity Masterchef*, earning her the 2014 Irish Tatler Woman of the Year award for Entertainment.

Dalkey Quarry is a long disused nineteenth-century granite quarry, thirty minutes outside Dublin city centre. A haven for walkers and rock climbers, and a sanctuary for wildlife including foxes and peregrine falcons, for Maïa Dunphy it's a picturesque place in which to take refuge and recharge . . .

I have been mesmerised by Dalkey Quarry since I was a small child. I grew up nearby: my parents moved to Dalkey a week before I was born. My mother was Spanish but raised in England and she had completely fallen in love with the area when driving around Dublin with my dad. It's where she wanted to raise us children. As a young one, my parents would bring me to the quarry in the pram and I began going up there on my own, or with my dog, from the age of nine or ten. You know as you get older how you value the friendships and faces of those people who've been around you the longest? The ones who know you intimately from all the before times? That's how I feel about the quarry. There is something reassuring about the familiarity of this view, one I've looked out on for most of my life. I've taken refuge in these rocks for as long as I can remember.

There are vertical steps cut into the side of the cliff. I find it useful therapy to climb them. I'm not terribly fit, and I get out of breath, but they take me out of myself and remind me of being alive. Since I was about sixteen, I'd take my dog Missy and my broken heart – unrequited love was a recurring theme for several years – and snacks and we'd just sit up there together. She died when I was twenty-two, and I

"I've returned to the quarry more often lately. I find it healing to be there."

"You know as you get older how you value the friendships and faces of those people who've been around you the longest? The ones who know you intimately from all the before times? That's how I feel about the quarry."

vividly remember the last two years of her life. Missy was riddled with arthritis and couldn't manage the steps anymore. So we kind of had an understanding. I'd say, "You wait here," then I'd run up and down the stairs and exhaust myself and we'd carry on a little more. I still miss that dog more than I miss a lot of people. I won't name any names.

I've a friend who does rock climbing in the quarry and he claims it's the best place to climb in Ireland. Now, I have no upper body strength to speak of, I can't even climb the monkey bars without my arms getting tired, but it's one of those things that I've thought about taking up as a hobby. Maybe see the quarry from some new perspectives.

There are all the obvious reasons why it's my perfect place: the quarry is as dramatic as it is beautiful and there's no better place to go when in need of greedy gulps of fresh air. If you stand at the very top, the view across Dublin Bay just takes the breath clean out of you. I love the poetic symmetry of the fact that you can see Dún Laoghaire pier from the apex because the granite for the pier was quarried from here.

I am not a gym or fitness person, but I have to get at least one walk somewhere every day. I am rarely the only visitor at the quarry – it's a very popular place – but it sometimes feels like I am. I try to go during the week, not at weekends when it can get very busy. When I am here I keep my headphones on and my head down, I try to pretend I'm all alone in this place of stories and stones and, for me, milestones.

So many milestones. That's the attraction of this place that's less obvious to the casual observer, the part only known and experienced by me. I've come here to mark various moments in my life. Exciting times, like when I had a book out. Or like when I was leaving to go travelling, to Borneo or Paris, I'd always go up to take a last, long look at the view. And I'd always be itching to go up there on my return too, as a sort of homecoming. After my marriage broke up, I'd sometimes leave my son Tom with his grandparents and go for long, head-clearing walks up the quarry.

I've returned to the quarry more often lately. If I'm ever sad, which I have been lately in the aftermath of my mother's death, I find it healing to be there. Even though she wasn't the biggest fan of the quarry because of all the stairs, I think about her all the time when I am up there. But I never want it to be a miserable place. It's been a gorgeous lifeline for me over the years and I feel very lucky because of that. I've gazed out at this same view since I was a baby and there is something deeply comforting in that continuity. And in knowing that this area is where my mother so dearly wanted us to grow up.

RÓISÍN MURPHY

ST JOHN'S WELL AND LYRE

RÓISÍN MURPHY is an actress from Dublin who played Princess Elsewith on History's drama series *Vikings*, recently appeared in the series *Miss Scarlet and the Duke* and received an IFTA nomination for Best Supporting Actress for her performance opposite Jack Reynor in Lenny Abrahamson's critically acclaimed film *What Richard Did*. Róisín trained at The Gaiety School of Acting and her film and television credits include *The Lodgers* directed by Brian O'Malley, *Our Unfenced Country* directed by Niamh Heery and Bobby Moresco's *The Hundred Code*.

Situated on the slopes of Mushera Mountain with sweeping views of the surrounding countryside, St John's Well in Co. Cork has long been a site of pilgrimage for Catholics. It's one of three wells in the area that are dedicated to the local Saint John of Mushera. Not too far from the well, Lyre village is in the parish of Clonmeen and is the highest village in the county, 266 metres above sea level. Róisín Murphy has strong family ties in this part of northwest Cork, which is what makes it her perfect place . . .

St John's Well is just at the foot of Mushera Mountain. The whole area around there is quintessential Irish countryside: rolling green hills for miles and miles. It's very high up and the locals say on a clear day you can see right out to the sea. I've never seen the sea from there myself, but I'll take their word for it.

I have a deep love for this area, a connection to it, for family reasons. My parents split up when I was quite young and my dad married a wonderful woman from the area. So from the age of seven I was brought to my stepmam's family in a tiny village not far from St John's Well called Lyre. There is no shop and no pub. It's as deep as you can get into rural northwest Cork.

Myself and my siblings were made so welcome there from the start. I think that's why it means such a lot to me. We were city kids. We stood out like sore thumbs, urban eejits looking for paths in the fields. We didn't fit in. But nobody ever made us

feel different. Our individual past and our lives in Dublin were acknowledged and we were very much welcomed into this new family when we came to visit. They made it feel so easy.

The whole area was the complete opposite of our background in Dublin, where we had a suburban upbringing by the sea. It was such a very different way of life. My dad and my stepmam had a daughter, Lil, my youngest sister. She's sixteen now and though she's so much younger than me we're very close. Because that part of the world is such a huge part of who she is, it gave me a whole new understanding of the place.

I have a vivid memory from years ago which captures how I feel about the area and my youngest sister. When Lil was making her first Holy Communion, she had this song and dance routine that her whole class had been working on. She'd been telling us about it for months. You could feel the excitement building. On her big day, she performed it for everybody in the church, delighted with herself.

Coincidentally, there was an engagement party for another family member that night. I remember we were moving off from the communion to this other celebration. Lil was aware her day was coming to an end; all the excitement was dwindling

"I can see her now, all excited and glowing with happiness, dancing up a storm on the mountain in her Holy Communion dress."

and she was deflated driving over to this other party. On the way, our dad said why don't we just stop at St John's Well to put a coin in it and mark the day. So that's what we did.

I don't know how it came about but we all decided to huddle together by the well, looking out at this incredible view; it was like something out of a storybook. That's when Lil, wanting to extend her big occasion, began to teach us the dance and song. We were all so much older than her, but she took the role of teacher because of course we hadn't a clue. As she instructed us in the moves, her excitement blossomed all over again and we got to share that moment with her. We didn't realise at the time how special it would be. I often think back on that scene, it was so innocent and perfect. I haven't talked to her about it in years, but it was a perfect representation of what that whole part of the world means to me.

My dad and stepmam moved away for a while nearer Dublin and then moved back to Lyre again. On my first trip driving back, after several years without a visit, I wondered once I went off the main road, would I be able to find my way? Google Maps doesn't work there. But even though it's all bushes and trees and countryside, I somehow remembered the way back to Lyre. It just came back to me, a reminder of how ingrained the place is in my life.

When I go down there it's a much slower pace than I'm used to after living in Dublin or Los Angeles. You can't help but switch off, even if you weren't intending to. I mean, you definitely don't want to go there to do any work, there isn't any broadband. And bring your waterproofs because it will most likely rain. The fog is spectacular sometimes.

I suppose it feels a bit like stepping back in time when I'm there. We go on family walks, there's lots of hiking and just being – if it doesn't sound too corny – "at one" with the landscape. A lot of the time we're just sitting by the fire and talking. Our days are based around meals, nice long breakfasts and lunches. It's all about being out in nature and then catching up around the fire, we hardly even watch the telly when we're down there. Because we don't see each other all the time, when we go there it's quality time with family and particularly with my little sister. I was the baby for so long in my family, now my relationship with her is such a joy. We never lived together: I grew up in Dublin and she grew up in Cork. She has chickens in her back garden, hens and cats and dogs and goats. She's a true country girl. Her love for her homeplace fed my love for the place too.

Despite our different upbringings, we are so similar. I never thought Lil and I would be so close but that's what has happened. I love that place because it means spending time with her and, of course, I have that special memory of her teaching us the routine at St John's Well. I can see her now, all excited and glowing with happiness, dancing up a storm on the mountain in her Holy Communion dress.

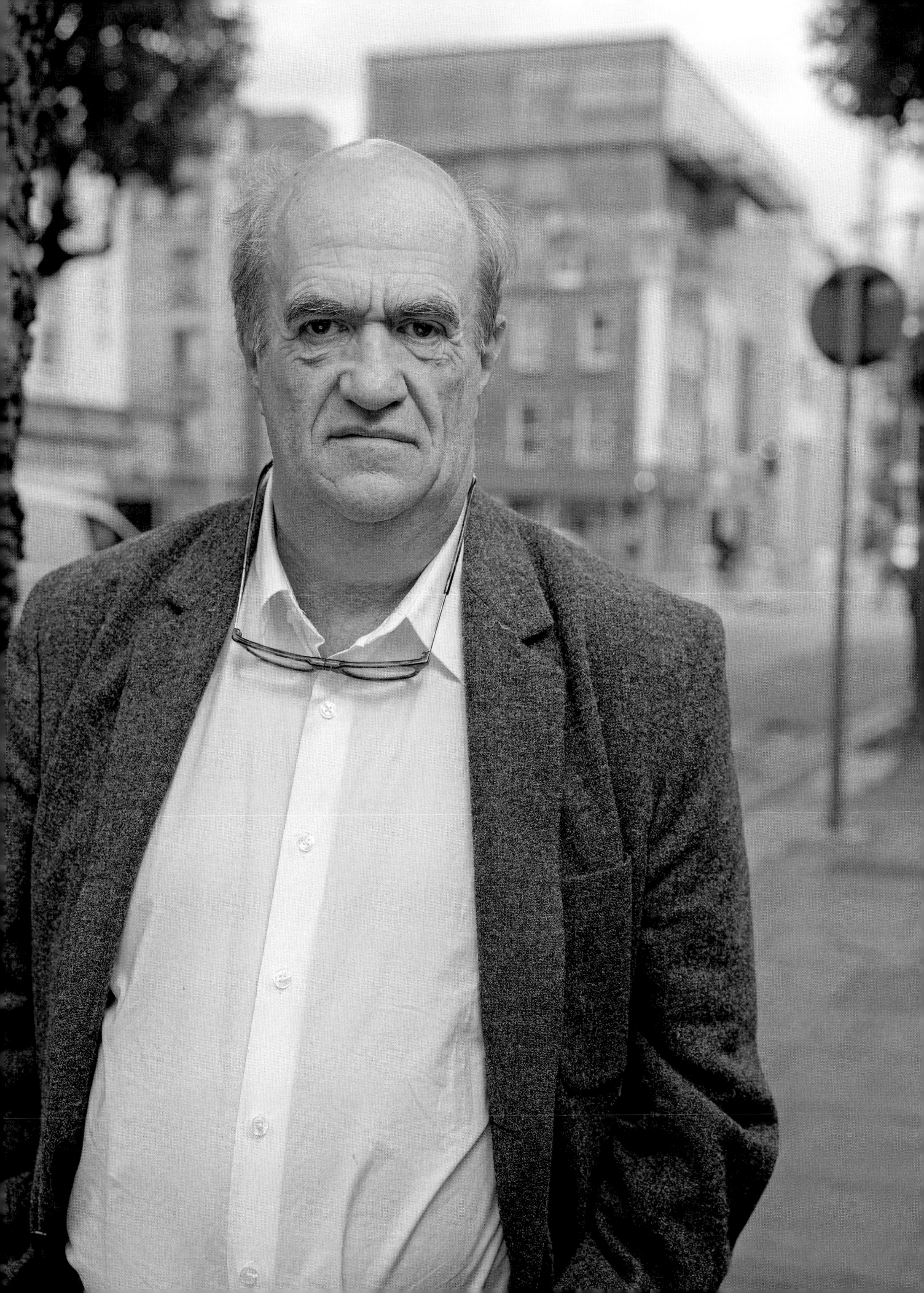

COLM TÓIBÍN

KELLY'S CORNER, DUBLIN

COLM TÓIBÍN is an Irish novelist, short story writer, playwright and poet from Enniscorthy, Co. Wexford. A graduate of University College Dublin, distinguished journalist and author of ten novels, he has been shortlisted for the Booker prize three times. His novels include *The Magician*, *The Master* and *Brooklyn*, which was made into an Oscar-nominated movie starring Saoirse Ronan. He is currently the Irene and Sidney B. Silverman Professor of Humanities at Columbia University and the third laureate for Irish fiction until 2024. He lives in Dublin and New York.

Kelly's Corner is one of several busy junctions in Dublin – like Baker's Corner or Edge's Corner – which still hold the name of the business that once operated from there, often a pub. This particular corner is at the busy junction between Upper Camden Street, Richmond Street, Harrington Street and Harcourt Road. For Colm Tóibín, a young man up to study from the country in the 1970s, it was a junction that bubbled over with possibility, a corner of Dublin that decades later still brings back vivid memories of youthful adventure . . .

In 1974 I was a student at UCD, fresh up from Enniscorthy. I had a terrible flat at the time, little more than a cell really, on Palmerston Road. I decided I didn't want to tolerate it anymore so I looked in the evening paper and found a tiny ad for a place in Hatch Street which was close to Kelly's Corner. The landlady was looking for a "professional gentleman", which I certainly was not.

Despite my lack of gentlemanly status, the landlady said I could come and look at the place. It was a room in the basement of a Victorian house with an outside toilet.

There was no bath or shower, but it was a large room in the back of the house with a garden. It cost three pounds a week. The landlady, who spent a lot of time on the phone to her friends and ran a poker school, ended up inspiring a character in my first novel *The South*. I somehow managed to persuade her that I was quite a serious person and would not be throw-

"Kelly's Corner was a celebration of everything urban. Completely unstable. Always changing."

ing any "student beer parties" as she called them. I got the place.

It was a really odd location for a UCD student to be living but when I started to explore the area, I realised it was perfect. For a nineteen-year-old country boy standing on Kelly's Corner, there was this vast sense of possibility, excitement and discovery. An abundance of choice is the whole point of living in a city and Kelly's Corner offered so many choices: there was the road that lead to Ranelagh over Charlemont Bridge, the road along the canal that leads up to Portobello going on to Rathmines or you could go along Harrington Street to Leonard's Corner, which would eventually lead you out to the Dublin Mountains.

When I moved to the area I realised my parents had kept something huge from me. It wasn't on the news, nobody had told me about this marvellous place called Camden Street. If you turned right on Kelly's Corner, you had Camden Street leading into Wexford Street, leading into Aungier Street, George's Street and then Dame Street. There were pubs everywhere and funny second-hand places, a street market and butcher's shops left over from another time. The place was filled with little shops that were newly opened or about to be knocked down and modern buildings that had just gone up, so the entire place was in a constant state of chaos, which I loved. On a Saturday morning, you got your newspapers and magazines and you could find somewhere to sit, looking out through a plate glass window at all the activity on the street.

As soon as you stepped onto Harrington Street from Kelly's Corner, it was exciting. This was an area where lots of Muslim immigrants had settled because that's where the mosque was and many of the buildings were still in flats so there was plenty of accommodation. It used to be "Little Jerusalem" but it had evolved into a sort of "Little Cairo". Wandering around was an assault on the senses, it was full of spices and strangeness. I found a launderette I could use on Curzon Street, which led to my discovery of those artisan houses on South Circular Road which were being done up, and of course I found the Jewish bakery. The area was also home to the most fashionable place to be in Dublin, the Manhattan Café, which was about as far from actual Manhattan as you could possibly imagine. It

“The landlady was looking for a ‘professional gentleman’, which I certainly was not.”

HARCOURT
ROAD

KELLY

was a grimy little burger joint open quite late, run by a really strict woman.

I suppose I could have got a better place somewhere else but it suited me. I never minded not having a bathroom because I had friends with nicer apartments and running hot water. Having no bathroom meant you could arrive at their place, inflict yourself on the most innocent person, demanding towels and soap and shampoo, and then lie in their bath for as long as you wanted. Luxury bath suds were big at the time. I have certain friends who since 1974 have avoided me because they think I will arrive in their house saying, "I've no time to talk to you, just give me a towel, let me have a bath and I'll see you next week." They couldn't really say no. I could have used the sports facilities in UCD but I had no idea where they were, having no interest in sport.

Kelly's Corner was a celebration of everything urban. Completely unstable. Always changing. Certainly not beautiful. Every building was ramshackle and different. It was pure urban decay and renewal. The decay continues. I remember on Harcourt Terrace, where I also lived, there was a huge Garda barracks and the Film Censor's office built by the OPW and designed in the 1940s by William Henry Howard Cooke and Oscar Leech. Both are owned by the State, both now derelict. Two buildings on the most beautiful terrace in Dublin boarded up because the State can't be bothered. This is what the Irish State thinks of the capital city. I look at it and marvel at the fact that they really, genuinely don't seem to care.

I lived in Hatch Street for a year and then went to Spain and friends took the room. When I returned it was available again so I moved back in. I remember the man in the front room of the house was a bachelor civil servant – I want to put him in a novel at some stage. He had not paid his ESB bill and had been cut off so he was living there by candlelight. Later on when the facts emerged, the landlady was appalled and asked "why didn't you tell me?" but I just assumed she knew.

All the time I lived there the landlady and I got on very well. I never did throw any of those "student beer parties" that haunted her nightmares. When I eventually moved I didn't go far. Kelly's Corner remained my hinterland and it is still the part of Dublin I am most drawn to now.

MIRIAM O'CALLAGHAN

DINGLE, CO. KERRY

One of the most popular public figures in Ireland, MIRIAM O'CALLAGHAN presents RTÉ's *Prime Time*, hosts her weekly *Sunday with Miriam* slot on RTÉ Radio 1 on Sunday mornings and presents a number of documentaries each year. She is also the first woman to present *The Late Late Show*, and won an RTÉ Guide Style Award and has two honorary doctorates from the University of Ulster and University College Cork.

Perched on the south-west Atlantic coast, Dingle is a small port town surrounded by some of the most arresting views in Ireland. From the quiet solitude of the Blasket Islands in Dingle Bay to the magnificence of Mount Brandon, the Conor Pass and Slea Head, the thirty-mile Dingle peninsula attracts tourists from all over the world. The town itself is full of character and each winter plays host to the internationally renowned Other Voices music festival. Long summer holidays in Dingle are fondly remembered by Miriam O'Callaghan . . .

My father was from the Kingdom so we went to Kerry religiously every summer for holidays. As anyone who has been there knows, Dingle is an extremely beautiful place but it also holds so many precious memories for me. I was there when my Leaving Cert results came out. We always rented a house on Green Street. I remember sitting outside on the front step of that house when I was sixteen years old, talking to my dad about what I might study in college. He thought I'd make a great doctor but I told him I didn't like blood. I ended up studying law.

So much of who I am is wrapped up in those holidays in Dingle. My parents were quite strict with us when we were growing up in Dublin but, perhaps because it was his home county, my father gave us much more freedom when we were in Kerry. We used to go to O'Flaherty's pub and stay there till four in the morning listening to

THE
LANTERN
B&B
HE LANTERN TOWNHOUSE
GUINNESS

"So much of who I am is wrapped up in those holidays in Dingle."

FOXY
IRISH WHISKEY
DUBLIN
ROE&CO
Y JOHNS
HARDWARE
DINGLE
Live
Streaming
Here
PALE

"I love the views in Dingle, the wide open spaces, the astonishing beauty of the land and sea."

music and having the craic. I'd go there with my sisters and I've so many precious memories from those holidays of my sister Anne. (Miriam's sister Anne died from cancer in 1995 aged thirty-three.)

One year, Anne fell in love with a gorgeous guy called Fernando. She was mad about him, which was brilliant because the Abba song "Fernando" was out at the time. You know the one.

Of course, I got stuck with Fernando's less gorgeous friend, which was what always happened on holidays.

When I had my own children, I kept going back to Dingle for holidays. During the summer we'd stay at the Dingle Skellig Hotel which, if you have lots of small children, is perfect. The hotel has a brilliant kids club which is included in your stay so it always meant my husband Steve and I could have a break and time to ourselves while the children were well entertained. We still go to the same hotel and my now adult children all walk past the kids club thinking about the happy times they spent there.

The other great joy used to be going out in a boat to see Fungie, the bottlenose dolphin who first took up residency in Dingle Bay in 1983. Boat trips to see him were always part of our holiday. We hadn't been out to see him for years when, during the summer of 2020, Steve suggested we all go as a family. This lovely fisherman took us out and my daughter was able to capture incredible video footage of Fungie jumping right up beside the boat. It was magical and made even more special by the fact that it was one of the last times Fungie was seen in Dingle Bay.

New Year's Eve is huge in Dingle – they have an annual parade which I would often launch. And of course, I've been down there for Other Voices, which was started by Philip King; another wonderful festival that put the town on the map.

I love the views in Dingle, the wide open spaces, the astonishing beauty of the land

and sea. It's definitely my special place. When I am busy, which is always, Dingle is where I can take a pause. I like to just stand and look out at the ocean and relax and breathe. I can be totally myself in Dingle. My husband Steve laughs because I don't really do much at all when we go there. It's a very simple holiday. I stay in the hotel or go for walks along the coast looking out at the ocean. All I really need is to breathe in the Dingle Bay air and that's me – I am happy out.

SO.935

IFRAH AHMED

ST STEPHEN'S GREEN

IFRAH AHMED is a Somali-Irish activist who is the founder of the United Youth of Ireland, a NGO providing support to immigrants and the Ifrah Foundation, which is devoted to eliminating FGM and partners with Amnesty International, UNICEF, and UNFPA to champion the rights of marginalised people. Ahmed advises the Somali government and the President of Somalia. She was awarded a People of the Year Award in 2018 and the film *A Girl from Mogadishu*, based on Ifrah's childhood, premiered at the Edinburgh film festival the following year.

St Stephen's Green in Dublin city centre is a park famous for its history, nature and a very busy children's playground. Entered by the Fusilier's Arch at the corner of Grafton Street, the park has statues commemorating various Irish figures from James Joyce to Robert Emmett. In one corner, at the south end of the central garden, there's a bust of Irish politician Countess Markievicz, who was a commander there during the 1916 Rising. The park's association with Markievicz is just one of many reasons why St Stephen's Green is Ifrah Ahmed's perfect place . . .

I first visited the park as a newly arrived refugee from Mogadishu in Somalia. As part of our English language classes, we were brought to different parts of Dublin and one of those was St Stephen's Green. I remember being struck by the natural beauty of the place, by the birds which were everywhere and by the stories our teacher told us about Countess Markievicz who was based with her regiment in the park during the 1916 Rising. As a woman and a feminist activist, her story resonated with me. The park felt like a special place from that time on.

I had arrived in Ireland in 2006 aged seventeen, escaping traffickers and eventually being granted asylum in Ireland. Soon afterwards I began campaigning for young migrants and for an end to female genital mutilation (FGM) in Somalia and elsewhere. I was a victim of this practice, where the genitals of young girls are cut with lifelong psychological and physical consequences. The UNFPA estimates that

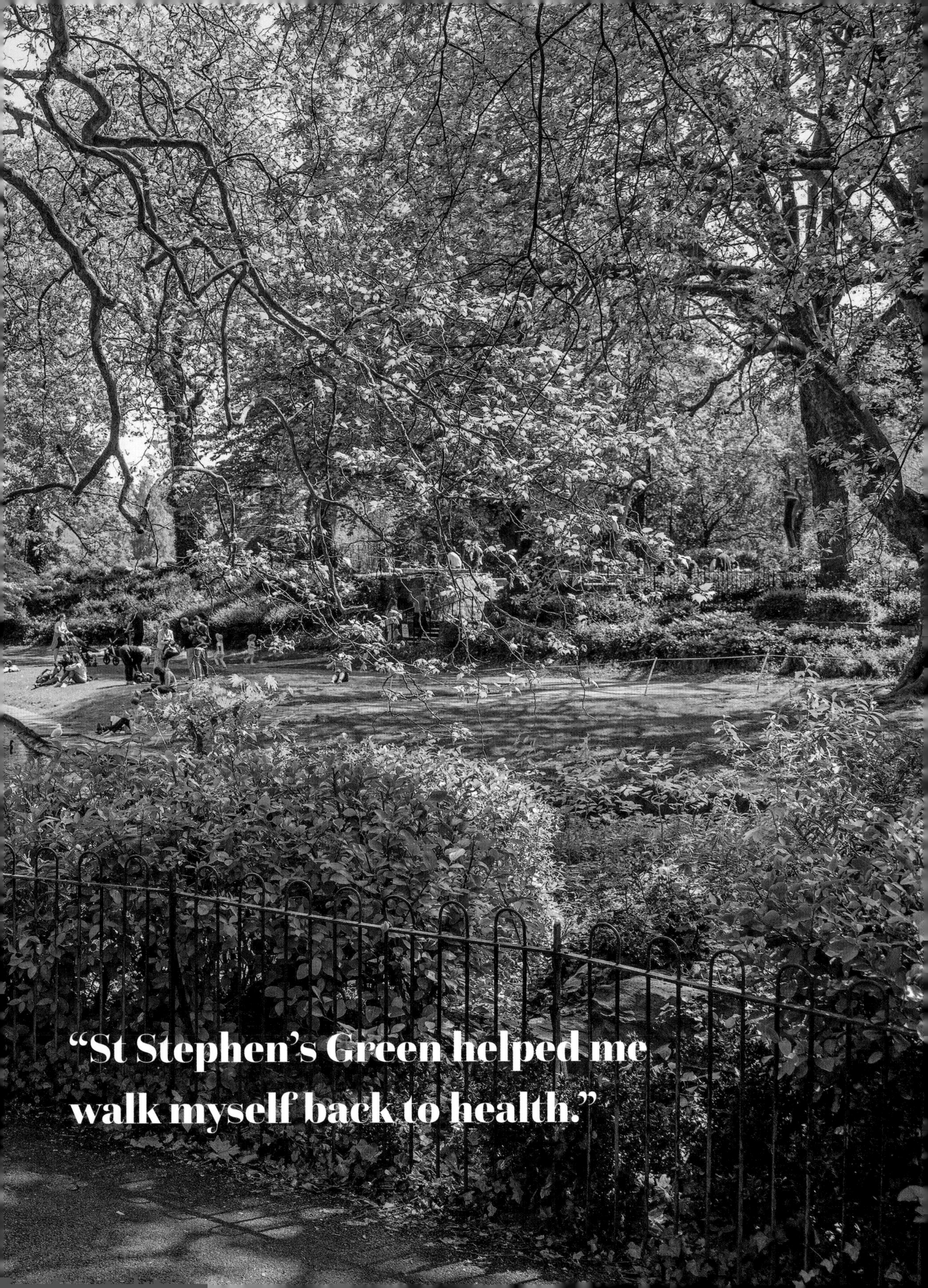
"St Stephen's Green helped me
walk myself back to health."

"Like many people, I found the pandemic challenging. St Stephen's Green was my saviour during that time."

200 million women and girls worldwide live with the after-effects of FGM, and Somalia has one of the highest rates in the world with approximately 98% of women and girls affected. FGM became illegal in Ireland in 2012.

As an activist and founder of the Ifrah Foundation, I describe myself not as a victim but as a voice. Becoming a voice has often meant being criticised. There were many people angry with me for speaking out against cutting, especially in Somalia. At those times, when anger was directed at me on social media or elsewhere, I would come to St Stephen's Green and sit in the solitude and peace of the park. It was my strength. It restored me back to myself.

Like many people, I found the pandemic challenging. St Stephen's Green was my saviour during that time. My daughter was born in January 2020, only a couple of months before the first lockdown. A friend was visiting from Somalia at the time, and she ended up getting stuck in Ireland unable to return home. We have a tradition back home that when a woman gives birth, she stays in bed for a long time and is looked after and brought food. I'd had my daughter by caesarean section, so my friend, with nothing else to distract her in lockdown, took this duty very seriously.

She cooked all the time, traditional Somali dishes and sweet treats, not allowing me to do anything except mind the baby. I gained a couple of what people now call Covid stones as a result and the weight gain affected my health, physically and mentally. When my friend went back to Somalia, I bought a set of scales and was a bit shocked when I stepped on them for the first time. I had also developed a thyroid issue.

St Stephen's Green helped me walk myself back to health. Every day I'd walk, with my daughter in the pram, from my home to the park. I started walking the circumference of the green. At first, I could only manage a few goes around, then five and by the end I was walking around it nine or ten times. Sometimes I'd walk along the canal all the way over to the Dublin Port offices and back. Dublin is a beautiful city for walking and there's no better place to go walking than St Stephen's Green.

In January 2021, my father died and I often went to St Stephen's Green to quietly grieve and reflect on his life. I am happy that, having been separated from my dad for a long time by war and geography,

we became close again in the few years before he passed away. He didn't fully understand or know about my activism, he was deeply religious and conservative, but he understood I was a humanitarian trying to help women. One time when I managed to visit him in Somalia despite the personal security risks which go along with my activism, he called me a "hero of heroes" because he had heard me speaking about my work on a British radio programme. This meant so much to me.

It was so horrible and heartbreaking that when he suffered a stroke during a fall, I could not travel to Somalia to visit him in hospital due to the security risk and the pandemic restrictions. But we were close at the end and that is comforting.

I've continued my campaigning work. It's my whole life. Initiatives such as the Dear Daughter campaign encourages mothers in Somalia to write a letter to their daughters, telling them how wonderful they are and making a pledge not to cut them.

My own dear daughter took her first steps in St Stephen's Green. She is a confident two-year-old now who knows what she wants. We'd often stop at Dunnes Stores on the way to the park to buy rice or dried fruit to feed the birds.

My daughter does not enjoy this so much anymore, not since the time a bird pooed on her head. Now she shoos them away and tells them "no, no, no!" when they come near. When I bring my daughter to the St Stephen's Green playground she loves it so much that it's often very hard to get her to leave. This can be frustrating but I have to smile at her protestations. I love this park too, so I know exactly how she feels.

NEIL McMANUS

RED BAY CASTLE, CUSHENDALL

NEIL McMANUS is a hurler who plays as a centre-forward for the Antrim senior team. Born in Cushendall, McManus has won eight Ulster titles, two Joe McDonagh Cups and one Walsh Cup, as well as six Antrim Championships and four Ulster Championships with Ruairí Óg. He joined a partnership between the RNLI and the GAA to prevent drowning and save lives by spreading water safety information. More recently, he co-founded Hurling at the Glens, where he shares the skills and history of hurling with visitors.

While perhaps less known than some of Northern Ireland's more popular tourist spots, one of the most impressive sights from the Antrim Coast Road are the ruins of Red Bay Castle. The majestic and storied ruins are part of Neil McManus's childhood and a perfect place he returns to often . . .

Red Bay Castle is in ruins now, but in the sixteenth century it was the stronghold of Sorley Boy MacDonnell – and the MacDonnells were the family that many of the Lords of Antrim and of Ulster came from.

Even earlier, this area and the western part of Scotland was part of the Kingdom of Dál Riada. The castle has an amazing view of Scotland on any half-clear day – you feel you could reach out and touch it. The family farm in Cushendall where our people came from was just behind the castle. I remember the first time I was brought up there by my mother and father: they were telling me the history, and it was going over my head. As a kid I played hurling with my brother and sister up there and I still have a photograph of us up there from about twenty-five years ago.

It was special. I always loved going to the castle, and even now if I'm out for a walk with my wife, Aileen, we'll always go and sit in there for a minute or two. I don't have a literary bone in my body, but

when I was ten, I wrote a poem about Red Bay Castle and it won a regional award. That's my claim to fame. My teacher lives nearby, and I often remind him of it.

There are three walls of it left standing now, but it's the green; the field it sits on seems to have the most green, plush grass you've ever seen in your life, and it's always so vibrant and bright. The lambs run in and out of the ruins, always gathering around the walls for a bit of heat or shelter. On your right, you can see the pier and the fishermen going in and out, and on your left, there's crystal clear water all the way to Scotland. Most days you can see Ailsa Craig, and on a really clear day you can see some of the Outer Hebrides. It's so visually spectacular that you don't think about anything else; you're just standing there in awe of the place. One year the Giro d'Italia came through and it was raining really heavily. My wife said we should watch it from under a tree for shelter, but I said this was the only place to watch it from.

It would be great to see the castle restored to what it was. Sorley Boy was the most famous of the MacDonnells; after him it fell into disuse but was restored again only to be destroyed by Oliver Cromwell in 1652. There's lots of folklore and history around this place, and there's a very famous storyteller called Liz Weir who's from the Glens of Antrim, who tells stories about the castle.

I've done a lot of travelling, but nowhere else feels more like home. And the castle is a great reminder of everything that has come before us, including how hard life

“The field it sits on seems to have the most green, plush grass you’ve ever seen in your life.”

“I’ve done a lot of travelling, but nowhere else feels more like home.”

must have been for the people here before the coast road arrived in the 1850s. This was the last fully Gaelic-speaking region of Ireland and I remember as a schoolboy going to the funeral of a lady in Glenariff who was the last person who had never spoken English.

It was because it was so hard to get in and get out – there weren’t really even roads, just paths and deep, glacial glens. They were essentially walking paths – a horse and cart would have struggled. And the locals had boats, so they could be in Scotland in half an hour if the winds and tides were right; if they had cattle and sheep to sell, they’d put them on boats rather than try to get them to market at Ballymena. Even now, I’m closer to Scotland than I am to a supermarket.

I lived in Belfast for six or seven years, but I was always going to settle here. Northern Ireland is brilliant now, because people are so free to express themselves in any way. I’ve spent a lot of time in Dublin as well with the GAA, and I see no difference between the north and south. We’ve got a great opportunity to make a brilliant society here in Ireland.

KEAVY LYNCH

DIGGES LANE DANCE STUDIOS

KEAVY LYNCH formed the band B*Witched alongside her twin sister Edele, Sinéad O'Carroll and Lindsay Armaou, selling over 3 million albums globally. Remaining active in the music industry, Keavy appeared in musicals such as *Snow White* and *Robin Hood and the Babes in the Wood* before becoming a qualified humanistic counsellor, opening her own practice and promoting mental health awareness. In 2021 the band launched their podcast *Starting Over with B*Witched* and have reunited to sing together again in preparation for their 25th anniversary in 2023.

Digges Lane Dance Studios in the centre of Dublin were set up in the 1980s, on the site of the former Kennedy's Bakery, which had lain vacant for many years. Apart from the studios, it provided facilities including a café, sunbeds, saunas and audition spaces. By 1994, when Michael Flatley began rehearsing Riverdance for the Eurovision interval with a troupe of Irish dancers, it was a dilapidated building, soon to be condemned. For Keavy Lynch it's a perfect place where all her dreams began . . .

My perfect place has long since been demolished. I can't go back there except in my mind. It's now a block of flats, on Digges Lane in Dublin. But when I was twelve, as a painfully shy, introverted young girl, Digges Lane Dance Studios were everything to me. I met myself there. I came out of my shell. I have such important memories of being able to express myself fully through dance and song. It's where I found myself for the first time and that might sound really sad, but it's the truth.

It was my older sister Tara who encouraged me to go there first. She noticed my dancing talent in particular and wanted to harness that. She got me to go to Digges Lane and I'm so glad she did because it was instrumental in everything I went on to do in my life. I went to so many classes there on Saturdays and Sundays.

“People used to ask us what we were rehearsing for and we’d say, ‘We’re rehearsing for our dreams!’ And we meant it.”

I did singing classes and all the dance disciplines – modern, tap, jazz and hip-hop. We did hip-hop with Mark (Sheehan) from the band The Script, who was our teacher, and Danny (O'Donoghue), also from The Script, was in our class. We actually formed a dance group together at one point called Boom. They were some of the best times of my life, with my twin sister Edele, making so many good friends and just hanging out together doing what we loved. The studios were near St Stephen’s Green. We’d rehearse there sometimes, and that whole area around the top of Grafton Street still means so much to me.

At first, my dad would drop me off at the studios and as I got a bit older, I’d get the 29a bus into town on my own. Eventually, I started to teach there and Digges Lane is where I met all the other members of B*Witched. Obviously, I knew Edele my entire life, but I met Sinéad (O’Carroll) there first. Sinéad and I became great friends and then one day she stopped talking to me and started talking to Edele. It turned out she didn’t know we were twins and thought we were the same person – I thought she had just ditched me for my sister.

It was Sinéad and Edele who started talking about forming a band, and then they asked me. We did some recording but we felt there was something missing. Another friend in the studios, Graham (Cruz), who is now a fashion designer and stylist, introduced us to Lindsay (Armaou) who was a singer and dancer and songwriter. We watched Lindsay in a dance class and thought, “Yeah, she’s awesome, she can dance and she seems nice.” Then we got her to sing a song for us and asked her to be in our band. It was all so innocent and easy and somehow we went on to make a worldwide career with our band B*Witched.

We did our earliest rehearsals for the band at Digges Lane. We all had day jobs. I worked as a mechanic in my dad’s garage so in some of our early photos I’m filthy, covered in oil. Then every night after work we’d go to the studios to practise. I remember people used to ask us what we were rehearsing for and we’d say, “We’re rehearsing for our dreams!” And we meant it.

Digges Lane closed down around a year or so before B*Witched had our first hit

LÁNA DIGGES
DIGGES LANE
2
GUINNESS

STREET
MULTI-STOREY
CAR PARK
P
OPEN
24 HOURS

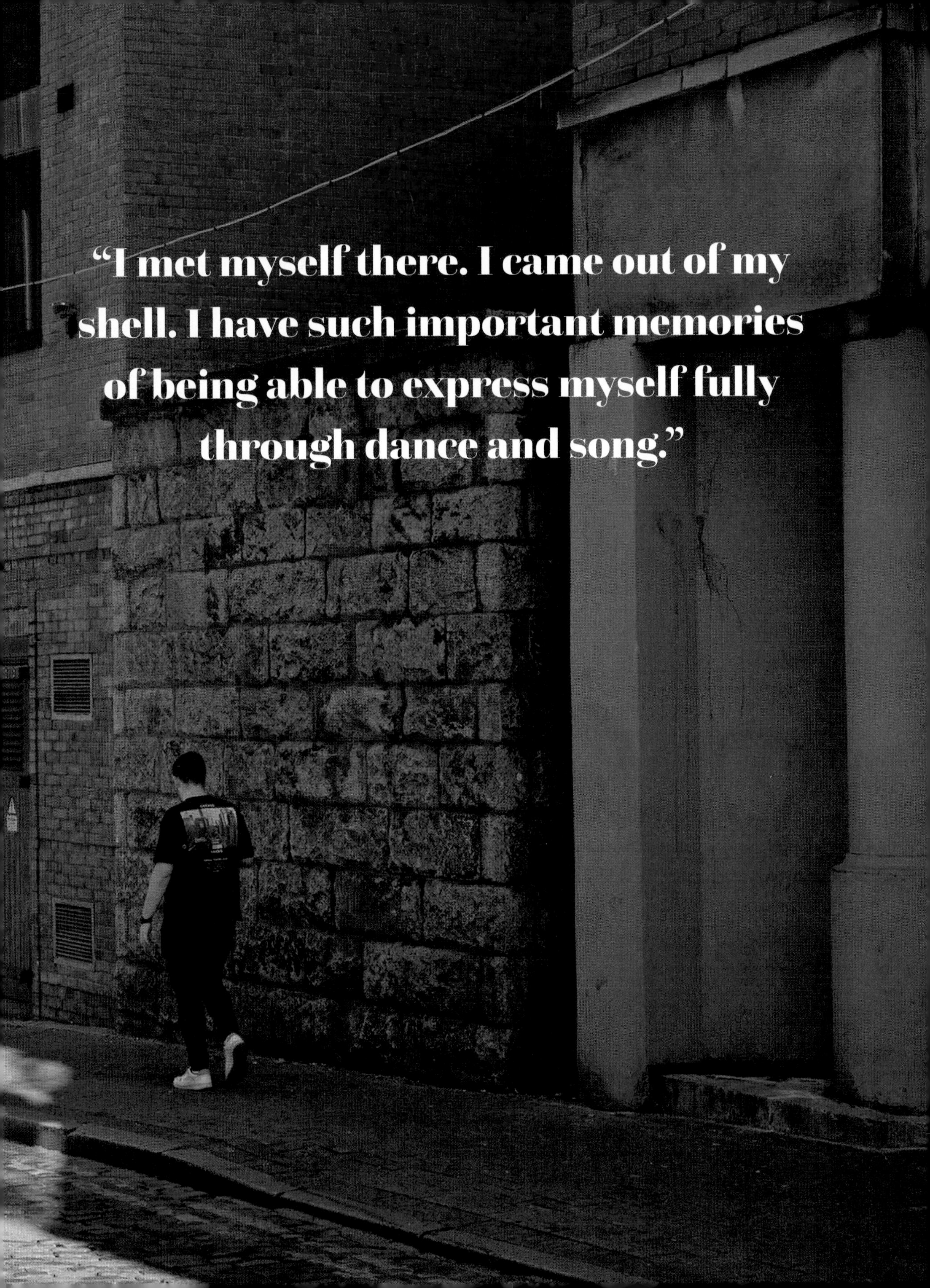

"I met myself there. I came out of my shell. I have such important memories of being able to express myself fully through dance and song."

single "C'est La Vie" in 1998. I went back the day it shut down. There were only a few of us there when the doors closed for the final time. I was devastated. I remember standing by the front desk, where we always used to hang out with whoever was answering the phones, just feeling really sad. I went around all the studios saying goodbye. It felt like the end of an era. I took a sign that used to be on one of the studio doors. I still have it in my mam and dad's garage, a precious memory from an incredible time and place that shaped the rest of my life.

THE HAIRY LEMON
LIVE
MUSIC
7 NIGHTS
A WEEK
LÁNA DIGGES
DIGGES LANE
2
THE HAIRY LEMON

TINA KELLEGHER

NARIN BEACH, PORTNOO

TINA KELLEGHER started her career working in Galway at the Druid Theatre. In 1994, she won awards for her portrayal of Sharon Curley in *The Snapper*. Kellegher then rose to fame joining the *Ballykissangel* series as Niamh Quigley, winning an IFTA for Best Leading Performance. She is also a familiar voice on RTE radio and BBC radio 4. She has continued on-screen acting in roles such as Ger Lynch in *Fair City*, appearing in the hit BBC 3 show, *Normal People* and the Irish film, *Herself*.

Narin, near Portnoo, is a small seaside village and townland in the parish of Ardara on the southwest coast of Co. Donegal. There is a large tourist trade served by several bed and breakfasts and caravan parks. Tina Kellegher has solid family connections in the area and years of childhood holiday memories which make it a place she keeps returning to . . .

The very first swimming lesson I ever had was at 9am on the beach at Narin with a cousin of mine. That's just one of thousands of childhood memories at Narin, but it's the family connections that mean the most.

There was history there. My paternal grandmother is from around Narin and Portnoo. We moved around a lot but I mostly grew up in Cavan. Daddy was a garage manager and so we followed his work around. The trips to Donegal were always so exciting. It wasn't one big trip a year, we'd be popping up a few times.

I remember long beach walks. It's over a mile of glorious sands, and rolling down the sand dunes for hours. You can walk out to the island of Inishkeel a little way off the coast of Narin but Mammy was always afraid of the tides so we never did it. There are the remains of two churches there, it's supposed to be where sixth-century St Conall Cael founded a monastery.

We used to rent a caravan. It was all about long summer nights and freedom and singing. When we got older daddy bought a caravan and his cousin, Dinny let him keep it in one of his fields. My

"I remember long beach walks. It's over a mile of glorious sands, and rolling down the sand dunes for hours."

"It's the family connections that mean the most."

father passed twenty-one years ago now and when I go to Donegal I always think of him. I just remember him laughing a lot. Donegal people love a laugh and he had so much fun with his cousins. We all did.

Mammy would produce three-course meals out of the caravan and the most amazing baking. We used to say, "Mam, you're on your holidays" but she loved it really. She'd be washing the windows and my grand aunt Bridie would say, "You'll bring the rain in washing those windows." When I think of Narin and Portnoo, I remember the smell of that gas cooker in the caravan, my mammy making spam on toast for us as a midnight treat and some of the best cups of tea you ever tasted. Perfect.

EAMONN COGHLAN
PHOENIX PARK, DUBLIN

EAMONN COGHLAN is a three-time Olympian and World Championship winning track runner. Born in Drimnagh, Dublin, he won four NCAA titles in the USA, set an indoor mile world record on three occasions and a world indoor record over 2,000 metres. He also won the famed Wanamaker Mile in Madison Square Gardens, New York, a record seven times. Eamonn has written an autobiography, *Chairman of the Boards, Master of the Mile* and was a senator from 2011 to 2016.

Located just a couple of miles from O'Connell Street, Dublin's Phoenix Park is the oldest walled park in Europe. Built as a royal hunting ground in the 1660s it was first opened to the public in 1747 and the park is home to Dublin Zoo, Áras an Uachtaráin, Victorian flower gardens and a large herd of fallow deer. A popular place for picnics, the sprawling park bustles with activity seven days a week as it fills with walkers, cyclists, polo players, cricketers and hurlers – not forgetting hundreds of joggers and runners, which is why it's Eamonn Coghlan's perfect place . . .

When I was a kid, every St Stephen's Day we'd go up the Phoenix Park to watch the Waterhouse Byrne Baird Shield, the oldest cross-country race in Europe, possibly the world. First held in 1896, the annual ten-mile handicap race is run by the famous Dublin athletics club Donore Harriers. My dad, a former runner, was friends with a lot of the runners in that club and took me to see the race from an early age. I always loved going along to watch, my breath foggy from the cold and cheeks glowing from all the Christmas Day feasting and fun the day before. Some of my fondest childhood memories are being up at the park watching runners of all ages and dreaming about doing it myself one day. I remember looking at the old timers who ran the race and thinking, one of these days I'm going to beat those guys. Many years later I did.

They called me the fastest kid on the block in the streets where I grew up on the Cooley Road, only a two-mile run from the park. There are 1,760 acres in the

Phoenix Park, which is about the same as the number of yards in a mile. A lot of my life and career is measured in miles – I earned the nickname "Chairman of the Boards" for my unprecedented wins on the indoor track – so there's a certain symbolism there. I've run many thousands of miles around the Phoenix Park from back when I was a young boy right up to this very day. I almost know every single acre, every blade of grass, every trail and every tree. I've always found peace and tranquility in the park but it's even more special because that is where I made my first mark as an athlete.

I joined Celtic Athletics Club, aged eleven, on a Sunday morning in 1965 because a boy in my class at school had joined. The club was based in the park and there was a one-mile cross-country race that day. The coaches were reluctant to let me run because it was my first time at the club. I cried at the injustice of it and got them to change their minds. When the gun went off, we made our way around the one-mile loop and into the trees. I'd been told to follow the leaders so that I wouldn't get lost. I passed some of the older lads running and they were calling me to come back. But I said "no, no, no" and kept going, just following the flags all the way around the forest. I ended up winning the race to the dismay of the officials.

Running gave me confidence and boosted my self-esteem. At school I struggled to memorise poetry and maths seemed incomprehensible. Later I discovered I was dyslexic but I didn't know it at the time. In my mid-teens I had a choice to make about which sports to focus on; soccer, GAA or running – I chose athletics. Because I got so much out of it physically and mentally and because winning races gave me such a high.

When Celtic broke up, the Metropolitan Harriers Athletics Club in the Phoenix Park approached me about joining and that became my club for most of the rest of my life, except for a four-year period when I joined Donore Harriers.

I joined Donore around the time I was studying at Villanova University in America. I'd come home and found there was nobody at senior level to train with. I wanted to train with people as good as and better than me. Joining Donore also gave me my first chance to run in the Waterhouse Byrne Baird Shield race that I'd watched for all those years as a child.

It's a handicap race for all ages and levels, the fastest person goes last while the slowest goes off first. So I was at home at 8.30am eating my breakfast, a small bit of tea and toast, when a man called Frank Cahill, aged seventy-eight, was the first person to start in the race. I had my breakfast, made my way to the park to do a little warm-up and was the last person to start running. I'm racing along and I'm catching up with everybody, passing them all out. With 200 metres to go on the main road of the Phoenix Park, who's in front but seventy-eight-year-old Frank Cahill. I ran as hard as I could to catch him but I didn't. I finished second. And

"Some of my fondest childhood memories are being up at the park watching runners of all ages and dreaming about doing it myself one day."

there was a caption the next day in the newspaper, something like, "Frank Cahill (78) outkicks Coghlan." Fortunately I came back the following year and won in record time, which still stands to this day.

Mostly when I think about the Phoenix Park I picture myself up at the Magazine Fort at the 15 acres. It's the spot that moulded me even though it was always mysterious and spooky to us as kids. It was originally built by the British in the 1700s but from 1922 until the 1980s it was a munitions store for the Irish Army. On each corner of the fort there is a tower and one of those towers was the start and the finish of the Munich Lap.

I was seventeen when the Munich Lap was invented. The Munich Olympics were coming up and our coach was trying to motivate us to become Olympians. He christened this three-quarter-mile loop the Munich Lap. It started at one of the

fort towers and took us out on a flat, then down a hill, up a hill, down a hill. It took in at least six short little hills over the distance of three quarters of a mile. It broke every stride we made, it would work your heart and work your lungs. The coach thought that if we could learn to "flatten those hills", as he put it, then we could become world champions.

I understood the philosophy. The Munich Lap tore us mentally and it hardened us physically. Coming off the last hill, you had to sprint like a madman for the last 200 metres. I bought into it, I believed it. And our coach was definitely on to something. In 1983 I won gold in the 5000 metres in the World Championships at Helsinki and finished fourth in both the 1976 and 1980 Olympics.

No other parks compare to the Phoenix Park, either for natural beauty or for training. When I lived in New York, I trained in Central Park but it didn't come close. The Phoenix Park just has more trails for a runner, more possibilities. If you do the perimeter trail, it's an eight-mile run. And you can build a ten, fifteen or twenty-mile run without repeating the same trails twice. The variety is superior to any other park I've trained in, including Hyde or Richmond Parks in London or Belmont Park in Philadelphia.

The park is also home to Áras an Uachtaráin where our President lives. When I became world champion I was invited up with my wife and children by President Patrick Hillery and his wife Maeve. Years later, when I came back from America, I befriended President Mary McAleese through my physical therapist Gerard Hartmann. He connected us because the President's husband, Martin McAleese, was keen on running and jogging. So the odd time I'd go over to Áras an Uachtaráin in my tracksuit. I'd meet Martin out the back of the house and go for a run around the park. Let's say he was able to keep up with me. Well, most of the time.

"I've run many thousands of miles around the Phoenix Park from back when I was a young boy right up to this very day."

ORLA KIELY

LOUGH DAN, CO. WICKLOW

ORLA KIELY is an internationally celebrated designer known for her iconic leaf print and retro graphics found on her dresses, accessories and household goods. She grew up in Dublin and her family ran Kiely's, a well-known pub in Donnybrook. Graduating in print and textile design from the National College of Art and Design in 1982, she and her husband Dermott Rowan established the Orla Kiely brand in 1995. The mother of two adult sons, she is London-based but always makes time for frequent trips home to Ireland.

Deep in the Wicklow Mountains, Lough Dan is a boomerang-shaped ribbon lake which, while set on private land, is popular with walkers who are free to explore the area. The lake is accessed via a gate located halfway between the Sally Gap and the village of Roundwood. The Wicklow Mountains National Park has many magnificent natural attractions but for Orla Kiely, Lough Dan beats them all . . .

There have been so many changes in Shankill, Co. Dublin where I grew up. The suburbs of the city are dramatically different from how they were when I was a child. The beginning of the walk to Lough Dan is only an hour from the centre of Dublin and a short enough drive from Shankill. This is a place that has not changed in all the years I've been going there. It feels like that anyway. I think that constancy is part of the reason I keep going back.

It's an annual thing for our family. When we're all home for Christmas, we'll get in the car and drive down, it's a sort of a pilgrimage. We get to blow off the cobwebs and spend quality time together. Once you are through the gate it's a two-hour walk downhill. There is nothing except nature. No car parks or cafés or any other signs of tourist life. You walk through this stunning landscape of mountains and streams and colour and it's an otherworldly experience. If you are lucky and end up there on a day when there's nobody else about it can feel like you are the only person in the world. I love that about some places in Ireland.

"As a landscape it's rocky and solid and raw and I like that. It's powerful."

Everything is vivid on that downhill walk. You see the yellows and purples of the mountains, the sky is vast and holds all sorts of colours depending on the day. The view is breathtaking. You might see a herd of deer or peregrine falcons. It's full of wildlife. You can see Lough Tay in the distance and whilst you can't see Lough Dan yet you know it's there waiting below. Finally, you get down to the lake, which is set into a valley. Looking over to the west there is Luggala and to the east Djouce Mountain.

Lough Dan isn't like any other lake I've seen. It's almost black, so dark it looks like tar. They call Lough Tay the "Guinness lake", because it's black and dark with a white sandy beach at the tip so it looks like a giant pint. But Lough Dan is also very dark at wintertime and quite stunning.

My two boys have been coming on this walk since they were children and now they are grown-ups and still love it. They grew up in London, which is great

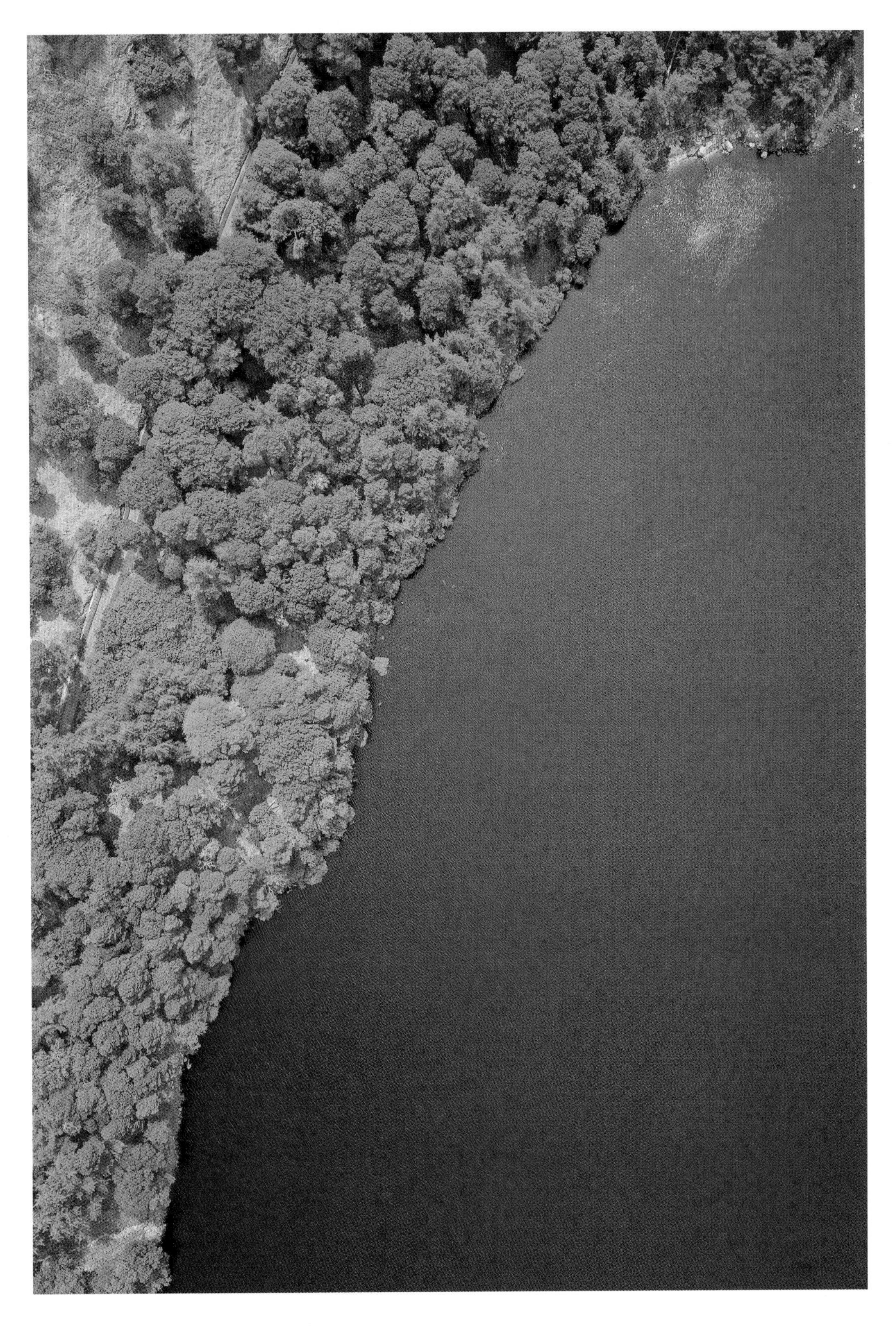

but very busy and they really value that space away from people, with nothing but nature and fresh air. We went twice last Christmas, I can't remember why. The first time it was a gorgeous still day and the second time the wind was phenomenal. I love that, being pushed and blown around the place. It makes you feel alive.

When you've been at the lake and taken in all the beauty, you then have to turn around and walk back. This is the challenge of it. You have to go back up that hill, and it can be tough but it's magical. We return to this walk again and again. The colour and the light are both very special. As a landscape it's rocky and solid and raw and I like that. It's powerful.

Over the years, Ireland has been important to me for colour. All those yellows and greys and greens – that bright orange in the hedgerows you see during the summer – enhancing that colourscape is what I do a lot in my work. My palette doesn't necessarily look Irish but it's definitely embedded in those colour families.

I don't know if it's possible to describe the beauty and magnificence of that walk to Lough Dan. I've always been a visual person. I get an emotional pang about certain places that's hard to put into words and I feel that pang when I think of the wild open spaces around Lough Dan. It's a place that just feeds my brain and my soul.

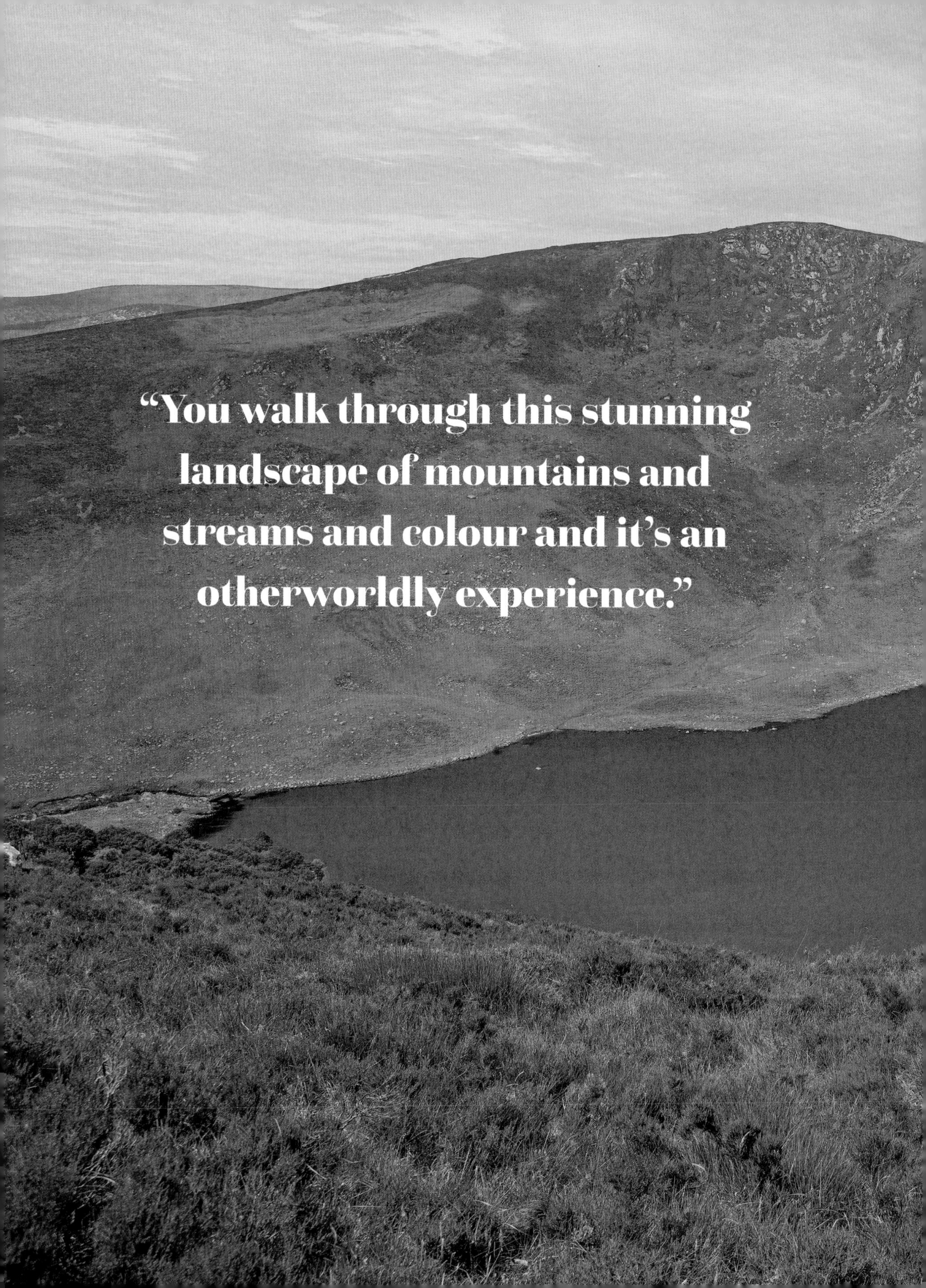
"You walk through this stunning landscape of mountains and streams and colour and it's an otherworldly experience."

DEIRDRE O'KANE
HOLY ROCK, DÚN LAOGHAIRE

DEIRDRE O'KANE is a stand-up comic, presenter and actress. As one of the Irish voice-over narrators of smash-hit TV reality series *Gogglebox*, she also starred in Darren Starr's hit sitcom *Younger*, and reached the finals of *Dancing with the Stars*. A co-founder of Comic Relief in Ireland, Deirdre helped raise more than 6 million euros for those most affected by the Covid-19 pandemic. She recently fronted her own talk show – *Deirdre O'Kane Talks Funny* – on RTÉ One alongside a new stand-up comedy series, *The Deirdre O'Kane Show*, on Sky.

During the interminable lockdowns, many of us discovered secret places in our local area as we walked around our 5k or 2k. "Holy Rock" is one of those secret places. It's near the popular Forty Foot swimming spot in Dún Laoghaire but Deirdre O'Kane won't tell us exactly where. She doesn't want anyone else finding out about her perfect place . . .

The absolute most I can tell you about Holy Rock is that it's around the corner from the Forty Foot. A lot of people don't even know it exists. And those of us who do know are scared to tell anybody because then they might go there and it wouldn't be as special anymore. I go there to meditate and drink coffee. Except when it's raining.

It was my husband Steve who found it on one of those lockdown walks around the area. He came home and said, "I've found this amazing little place." So the next day he showed me and we went together. I couldn't get over the views of the sea, how remote it felt.

The fact that on my way to this place that didn't feel like anywhere close to civilisation I was able to buy a takeaway coffee blew my mind. I sit in amazement on that little rock and the coffee is central to the experience.

I have a great love for the sea. I find it very healing. I need a daily fix of water. When we lived in London we lived near a river. But the sea really does the business. I breathe better when I know I can get to

“You sit there and all you can see is the sea.”

it quickly. And I need to be able to get to it quickly, which is why we moved to Dún Laoghaire.

I'm not going to lie. I am deeply envious of the people who have very fancy houses that look directly over the coast but there's something amazing about the fact that you don't actually have to have the fancy house. You can still reach these paths and these places, you can still get access to stunning viewing spots like Holy Rock where you are opened up to the vast expanse of Dublin Bay. You sit there and all you can see is the sea.

I meditate there, which is why we call it the Holy Rock. I do Transcendental

Meditation but all meditation is the same really. You have a special word you say to stop all the noise and it works for me. As with everything else, though, I will lapse. If I'm on a diet, I'll break it or if I commit to something good for me, I'll do it for a bit and then lapse. I'm the same with the meditation but I don't do well when I lapse so I try to keep it going every day. I'm a nicer person when I'm meditating. I'm better at everything across the board. I wasn't blessed with patience so I have to work on that and the auld meditation helps.

If I told you where Holy Rock was I'd have to kill you but I suppose I can tell you that you get to it at the end of a private road, an ordinary residential road that you'd never guess was the way to such a wonderful place. You'd have no business on the road unless you knew somebody who lived there. Then you go through a gap and down some steps and there it is. I'm always expecting other people to be there but it's rare that you'd see anyone because it's only really big enough for a couple of people. And if someone does come along, they usually say "oh sorry" like they feel terrible for disturbing you on Holy Rock and they slink off. And I can't believe it. I just can't believe I can walk fifteen minutes from my house and be in a place like this. We could be in the west of Ireland or the south of France or Sicily but we're not, we're just down the road from our house in south Co. Dublin.

Do I swim there? God, no. Do I look like a Dryrober to you? I can't do it. I'd rather tell jokes to 5,000 strangers than get into that water, it's just too cold for me. But I'm happy to let other people throw themselves in the sea while I sit there with my eyes closed sipping coffee in a secret, sacred place.

"We could be in the west of Ireland or the south of France or Sicily but we're not, we're just down the road from our house in south county Dublin."

PROFESSOR LUKE O'NEILL

THE LONG ROOM, TRINITY COLLEGE

LUKE O'NEILL is professor of biochemistry at Trinity College and is a leading scientific commentator on Covid-19. He has a weekly science slot with Pat Kenny on the Irish national radio station *Newstalk*, and has won multiple awards and fellowships, including the An Post Irish Book of the Year Award for *Never Mind the B*ll*cks Here's the Science,* one of his four books written to bring science to life for the general public. He was also given a Science Communicator of the Year Award for his work during the pandemic.

Built between 1712 and 1732, the Long Room in the Old Library of Trinity College Dublin is probably one of the most famous libraries in the world. Measuring almost sixty-five metres in length, the room is located on the north side of Fellows Square and contains 200,000 of the college's oldest books including the legendary Book of Kells. The Long Room is Professor Luke O'Neill's very conveniently located perfect place, a ten-minute stroll from his office . . .

I've brought so many people to the Long Room during my time at Trinity College Dublin. As a senior member of staff, I am one of the people who gets to show visitors around. They all gasp when they walk up the stairs and gaze at that barrel-vaulted ceiling. This is a room that never disappoints.

The most famous person I helped to host was Queen Elizabeth II in 2011. I got to know the Queen in that room. She walked towards me, I shook her hand and introduced her to six colleagues. We chatted for about twenty minutes. I remember the Queen staring in awe at the gold lettering in Latin on the ceiling which marked a seventeenth-century donation to the university from King Charles II. She also

"These are great treasures of our civilisation."

spent ages looking at a parchment which bears the signature of Queen Elizabeth I – she was the original donor when Trinity was established in 1592. She was really taken with it. To be honest I hadn't much interest in the Queen before, but she was so sharp and so well briefed that after meeting her I thought: "What an impressive woman."

When it was built in the early 1700s, the Long Room was the biggest library in the world. Even today it's the envy of places like the Smithsonian and when I've visitors from Harvard University I tell them, "Our library beats yours." It's very competitive on the library scene, you see. For a scientist, Trinity's library is hugely important in terms of the books you will find on the shelves. There's a first edition of Darwin's *Origin of the Species* and a first edition of Newton's *Principia*, which contains all those discoveries about the universe and gravity and the laws of planetary motion. These are great treasures of our civilisation.

It's not like a regular library: it's been a museum since the mid-nineteenth century and you need a specific academic reason to seek permission to look at the books. Years ago, when I was a student, a friend was studying zoology. He wanted to do a project on a particular species of spider, so he was looking for a book from the 1800s. He got the book out and discovered that the wax seal had not been broken. It turned out he was the first person to ever look at the book. Nobody else had ever read it. I felt sorry for the author.

The books are now being digitised, which will be a tremendous resource for scholars. I feel very lucky that I got to launch my first book, *Humanology*, in the Long Room, with the librarian's permission. That's some overreach getting to launch my book here considering the quality of the texts that are on the shelves.

Aside from those ancient and exciting books, including the *Book of Kells* downstairs, which everyone knows about, the Long Room contains many other treasures. There's a very rare copy of the *1916 Proclamation*, for example. And there's a harp made from oak and willow that's the oldest in Ireland; they think it dates from the 1400s. That harp inspired our national emblem. I always tell visitors the story of how Guinness asked for permission to use the same harp as their trademark in the 1850s. Apparently the college said yes but wanted some quid pro quo, which is why, since then, a barrel of Guinness is delivered every week to the college.

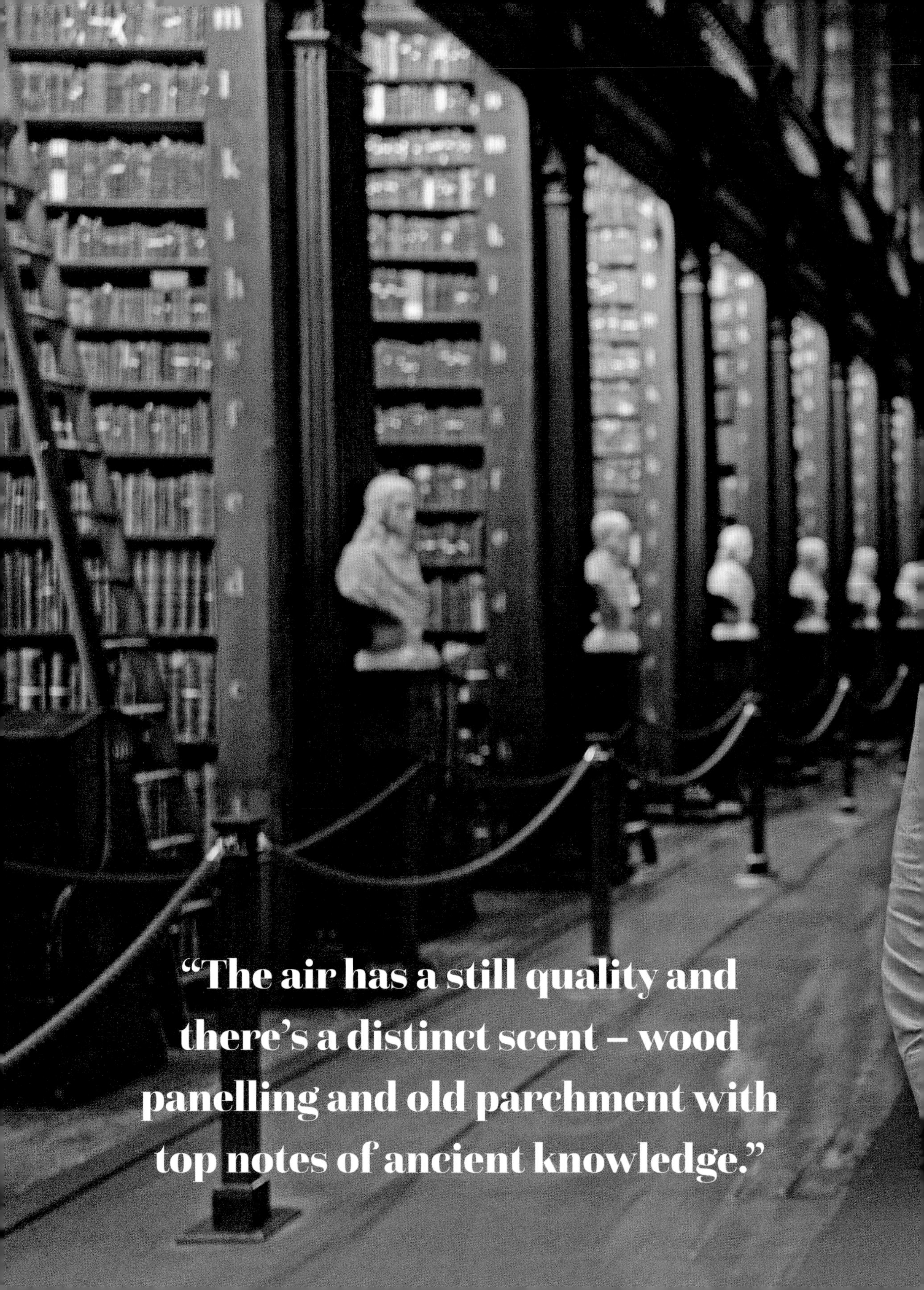

“The air has a still quality and there’s a distinct scent – wood panelling and old parchment with top notes of ancient knowledge.”

Along with the books the place is full of ghosts. The ghost of a Trinity fellow who was killed on the campus allegedly haunts the book stacks. There are also forty marble busts of philosophers and writers, from Socrates to Shakespeare, on display. Of course they are all men, including some former fellows of Trinity that nobody has ever heard of. I'm glad to say that in 2020 four busts of women were commissioned: mathematician Ada Lovelace, theatre-founder and folklorist Augusta Gregory, scientist Rosalind Franklin and women's rights campaigner and writer Mary Wollstonecraft. These were the first commissions of busts in more than a century and I'm glad that imbalance is being addressed.

If I was to try to persuade someone to visit who had never been, I'd tell them the Long Room is visually stunning, like something out of *Harry Potter*, an architectural gem. But what's more difficult to describe is the unique atmosphere. The air has a still quality and there's a distinct scent – wood panelling and old parchment with top notes of ancient knowledge. Maybe it's the serene feeling I get when I am there but I've always found it a great place to recharge the batteries and it brings me such joy to show it to visitors – royal or otherwise. Sometimes I like to go there at around five in the afternoon, when the early evening sun is slanting through the windows. There's a special feeling in that room that I just don't find anywhere else.

ii
hh
gg
ff
ee
dd
cc

ARMS HOTEL

SENATOR EILEEN FLYNN

THE DIAMOND, ARDARA

After years of activism focused on issues of equality and access that affect her community and the larger society, Eileen Flynn became the first Traveller in the Oireachtas in June 2020, when she was nominated to Seanad Éireann by the Taoiseach. That year, the BBC named Flynn to its list of 100 inspiring and influential women from around the world. Flynn continues to advocate for her community as chair of the Joint Oireachtas Committee on Key Issues Affecting the Traveller Community, and for a more equal and inclusive society for all.

All across the province of Ulster there are "diamonds" in the centre of towns or villages. The Diamond in the heritage town of Ardara, Co. Donegal is one such place. This is where the Christmas lights are switched on, where people gather for commemorations and where locals and visitors come to people-watch or shop. One of Ardara's most famous sons, John Doherty, is commemorated with a statue by Redmond Herrity in the middle of the Diamond. Doherty, a member of the Traveller community, was one of the most revered Irish fiddlers of the twentieth century. Eileen Flynn, who moved to the town in 2018, comes to the Diamond to reflect on identity and belonging.

The first time I went to Ardara was in 2017 with my then boyfriend, now husband Liam, who is from the area. We were sitting in Nesbitt's Boutique Hotel on the Diamond having a bit to eat and we were telling each other more about ourselves. We'd been friends for a good while but hadn't been together too long romantically at that stage. We were just eating and chatting away when I noticed the statue outside in the Diamond.

I thought it was a funny-looking piece of art, if I'm being honest with you. The man, a musician, had no arms and half a fiddle on his shoulder. Liam said, "Well, I don't know what that's all about, Eileen, but he's Johnny Doherty, a famous fiddler

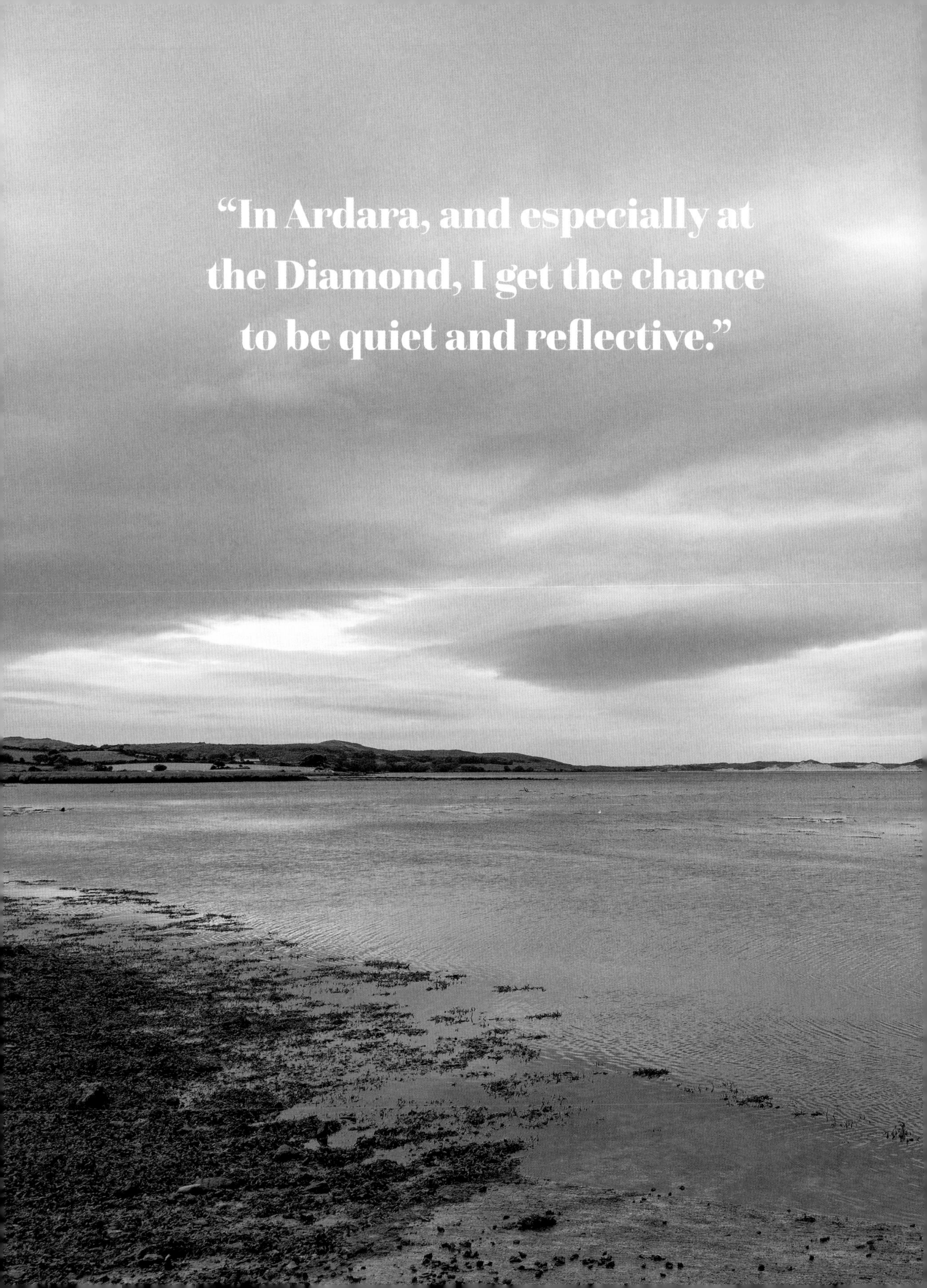
"In Ardara, and especially at
the Diamond, I get the chance
to be quiet and reflective."

and a member of the Traveller community." There was something so special about that moment. I think it was the fact that when I saw it, I was telling Liam about my own background being a Traveller.

Obviously there is prejudice and discrimination everywhere, however when I saw that statue it made me think there must be loyalty and solidarity towards Travellers in this place if they had a sculpture like that in such a prominent location in the town. Also, as far as I know, John Doherty is the only Traveller in Ireland that has been commemorated with a statue. So the Diamond has been a very special place to me since that day.

Ardara is my home now, the place where Liam and I are raising our children. I'm thirty-two but I spent the first twenty-eight years of my life on a halting site in Ballyfermot in Dublin. Labre Park in Ballyfermot is another one of the best places in the world to me. It holds so many memories, growing up there with my mam and dad, both of whom have passed now, and my eight brothers and sisters. We'll still gather in that house for family get-togethers but these days we bring our own children and there might be twelve kids running around that tiny house, including my two small daughters, Billie and Lacey.

BREWERS, MALTSTERS
ROBIN
TRADITIONAL
HOT WATER STARCH
FOR AN EXTRA CRISP FINISH
J&B
SCOTCH WHISKY
TAYLOR
WALKER
IRISH STOUT
PLAYER'S
BROWN FLAKE

I'm a blow-in to Ardara at the end of the day, which has nothing to do with my Traveller roots – I'm a blow-in because I'm a "Dub". That's why it meant a lot to me when the town came out to celebrate my nomination to the Seanad. The Diamond is also a great place for people watching, especially in the summer when the music is spilling out from the pubs and life is going on all around you. The Diamond can also be a place to gather when people are hurting, as the community did early this year to remember Ashling Murphy.

Since I became a senator in June 2020, I've been working in Leinster House. I leave Ardara on Sunday or Monday, but always look forward to coming back to the town on Thursdays or Fridays. In Dublin I am busy, it can be chaotic always running about and going to meetings, but in Ardara, and especially at the Diamond, I get the chance to be quiet and reflective. I enjoy both – the hectic pace of the city and the calm of Ardara. That peace and quiet is important, especially as I suffer with my mental health and anxiety. I look at the statue of John Doherty and it feels grounding. I never want to forget who I am and where I come from.

People in the town would be very aware of my background. I've been welcomed so warmly and have so many friends, especially young people, around the area. I'm very relaxed here. I'd go out around the town in my blue crocs and my stockings and not worry about what anyone might think of me. I can be myself, just Eileen.

I remember one time shortly after I was married, a man in the local pub said to me, "What do you think of Ardara?" I told him the town reminds me of one big Traveller halting site. I don't think he was expecting that. But what I meant was that it reminded me of home, of Labre Park, and of the caring nature of the community. Adara makes me think of Labre because there is such a strong sense of community, family and belonging here, with the Diamond at the heart of it.

"I look at the statue of John Doherty and it feels grounding. I never want to forget who I am and where I came from."

PAUL HOWARD

CROMLECH FIELDS, BALLYBRACK

A journalist, author and comedy writer, PAUL HOWARD spent sixteen years working for the *Sunday Tribune* as an award-winning sports journalist before creating the "rugby jock" character Ross O'Carroll-Kelly, whose adventures have been the subject of twenty-one novels and three other books that have sold over 1.5 million copies in Ireland. Alongside becoming a record four-time Irish Book Award winner, Howard also writes for theatre, film, radio and television and was the subject of the RTÉ documentary, *We Need to Talk about Ross*.

Located in Ballybrack, Co. Dublin, Cromlech Fields was a housing estate built in the late 1970s when the economic recession and high unemployment meant there was significant demand for local authority homes. The council estate was named after a Cromlech (or Dolmen), an ancient stone portal tomb that sits in the middle of the estate and dates from 2500 BC. For several years the housing estate was Paul Howard's playground . . .

Cromlech Fields is the housing estate where I grew up and it's where I've been happiest in my life. It's just the mad abandon of the place. You could walk out the front door and anything could happen. You could get punched in the face, you could score the winning goal in a match or somebody could ask you to mow their front lawn and you might get two quid.

The highest praise anybody could have given me back then was to call me a daredevil. There was a bull in a field nearby and sometimes we'd go for a chase off it. We'd jump into the field and start antagonising the bull until he started running at you. It was all about being the last person to run away from the bull, seeing the whites of his eyes before you ran.

Our family had moved back to Dublin in 1979, from Luton, England, where I'd been born and where we lived in this huge Irish community. My dad had this idea that Thatcherism wasn't going to be good for people like us, a working-class Irish family, raising four boys under the age of ten and relying on a manufacturer's wage. My dad told us before the 1979 election that if the Tories won we would be moving back to Ireland. We thought he meant it in

“I remember coming home after a day out playing, covered in mud from head to toe.”

"You could walk out the front door and anything could happen."

the way people said if Trump got elected they were moving to Canada, an idle promise. But we came home from school one day and my mother was packing all our stuff into boxes.

We didn't have a house yet in Dublin, so at first we lived with my granny. The end of the rainbow was going to be the council house in Ballybrack. We moved there in December 1980, the week John Lennon died.

Cromlech Fields is in Ballybrack, which is very close to Killiney, so as kids we used to look up at Bono's house on the hill. It was the first million-pound house we'd ever heard of, but it couldn't have been further away from us in terms of status.

Our house was 122 Cromlech Fields. I went back there to film something a few years ago and the woman who owns the house now couldn't stop talking about what a brilliant house it was, so solid and warm. The estate was one of about six that were all adjoined. They were really well-built homes. I've lived in private houses since. The walls are paper thin but the houses in Cromlech Fields were built to last.

Ours was a big red brick corner house with a side passage and a long garden. They gave out the houses on a points system as they were built, depending on each family's need. When we moved in, most of the houses on the estate were still being built. For the next couple of years the building site was our playground. We'd do dares. Climbing up on scaffolding, going down manholes. It was brilliant, highly dangerous fun. I remember coming home after a day out playing, covered in mud from head to toe.

There were such a mix of people on the estate. They came from all sorts of backgrounds. You could find members of the Travelling community, families down from the North to escape the Troubles and a few unaccountably posh people who had somehow ended up there. We also met Vietnamese refugees – they started the first fish and chip food vans on our estate. When I think of my childhood in Cromlech Fields, I think of winter nights with fog on my breath, the smell of smoky coal and chipper vinegar mixed with grease.

There was no infrastructure at all, no shops, so everything came out of vans.

As well as the chip van there was the shop van which was run by a guy called "Dave Shop Van". That sold everything you could possibly need – bread, milk, single cigarettes. Our library was a van, it came around the estate every week. We'd borrow our books and then rock the van back and forth for fun.

The council built a load of houses in the area but nothing else. They left it to the people to build a community. What really shaped that community was the culture of volunteerism. We went on summer projects, all run by volunteers, mostly women who lived on the estate. They gave up their time so we could have a good summer. We got brought to the zoo, to the beach, they organised coach trips. It was women like that who created our community and breathed life into the place. Otherwise, it was just houses.

When I go back to Cromlech Fields I'm instantly transported to my childhood. I know every part of it intimately. There's one hill we used to go down on a shopping trolley that we turned into a go-kart. You couldn't control the wheels so it always ended up with somebody getting their head split open. I know every bump on that hill.

I have photographic recall of certain days. I remember we were putting a rope bridge on a tree one day and my friend Jason was up on the branch singing "Making Your Mind Up" by Bucks Fizz who had just won the Eurovision at the time. I have a visual for that day and I know how that day sounds. The sense memories are still so strong.

Back then local authority housing was built to meet a need: there was a huge demand and in the middle of a recession the government found money to build houses for people. They looked after people who couldn't afford to buy their own homes. The government realised this was a social emergency and responded to that emergency. It doesn't happen to the same extent now and that's wrong. It's why we have a housing crisis.

I was sixteen years old when we moved out of Cromlech Fields. At some point the council sold all the houses and people living in them got a chance to buy them really cheap. I wanted to buy a house there twenty years ago but I couldn't afford it.

I still go back. I'll walk around just remembering stuff, maybe go over to the Cromlech, which is smack bang in the middle of the estate. We were told in school that a king was probably buried underneath it. One night a gang of us kids decided to dig it up to find his treasure, but we got spooked in the end. The real treasure for me is all the memories I have of that very special place.

ANNE ENRIGHT

KILLINEY HILL

ANNE ENRIGHT is a multi-award winning writer whose novel *The Gathering* won both the Booker Prize and Irish Novel of the Year. She has written two collections of stories, published together as *Yesterday's Weather*, one book of non-fiction, *Making Babies*, and six novels. A Fellow of the Royal Society of Literature, she also won the first ever Andrew Carnegie Medal for Excellence in Fiction for *The Forgotten Waltz*. Born in Dublin, where she now lives and works, Anne's writing explores a wide variety of themes including love, death, sex, motherhood, family relationships, culture in present-day Ireland as well as the country's complicated socio-political history.

The spectacular views from Killiney Hill attract walkers from all over the city. On a clear day you can see the mountains of Wales to the east and Bray Head and the Wicklow Mountains to the south. Anne Enright is a regular on the hill and got to know the landscape more intimately during the pandemic . . .

It was something that happened during those dreaded lockdown walks. Putting one foot in front of the other on the path up Killiney Hill. It was a cumulative thing; it felt as though I was seeing everything differently. I was micro-focused on the fronds of the ferns and walks there became quite a poetical, mystical event. But then you'd get grumpy again of course. Nothing was changing. Here we were again, still in lockdown.

It was a peculiar time. The world had gone strange and yet the weather was so beautiful during that first lockdown, and that perversely was so enjoyable.

The place on the path that I liked most is a bowl of rock, a little valley that seems to cook up the gorse. Now, I am not a huge fan of gorse. It's too coconutty. But my da used to love gorse and he'd say, "oh, the gorse is out" and I used to think that was the most boring thing anyone could ever say. And then you'd have to go up the Dublin mountains with him to look at the gorse on a Sunday afternoon. But on those strolls up Killiney Hill, I started kind of getting into the gorse.

At the end of the dell there are the steps and they are the steps of doom. Because

however many times you have to stop on those steps is a sign of how fit or not you are on that particular day. They go up five storeys. They are not steps for the faint-hearted. And you'll always meet people there.

Then you get to the top. That view of Dublin Bay in the time of lockdown especially seemed momentous, knowing you were looking down on all the people in the city people in their pods and bubbles. And you know the rocks dug out of the quarry below were turned into Dun Laoghaire pier by Captain Bligh no less. So it feels like primary school, somehow, you get your history and geography lesson right there.

By the end of lockdown I'd done the hill in every possible variation and never got bored. That dell felt and does feel like an amphitheatre, there is a sense of story, and you are aware of your smallness in the landscape. Seeing the ferns as they unfold and noticing that now it's the time for the buttercups. You become interested in how it all changes week on week. That suspense of waiting for spring or other seasons to come, that sequence is important. It became such a daily ritual. Seeing those tiny changes. All the sudden growth and unfurling. We never get tired of it.

"Walks there became quite a poetical, mystical event."

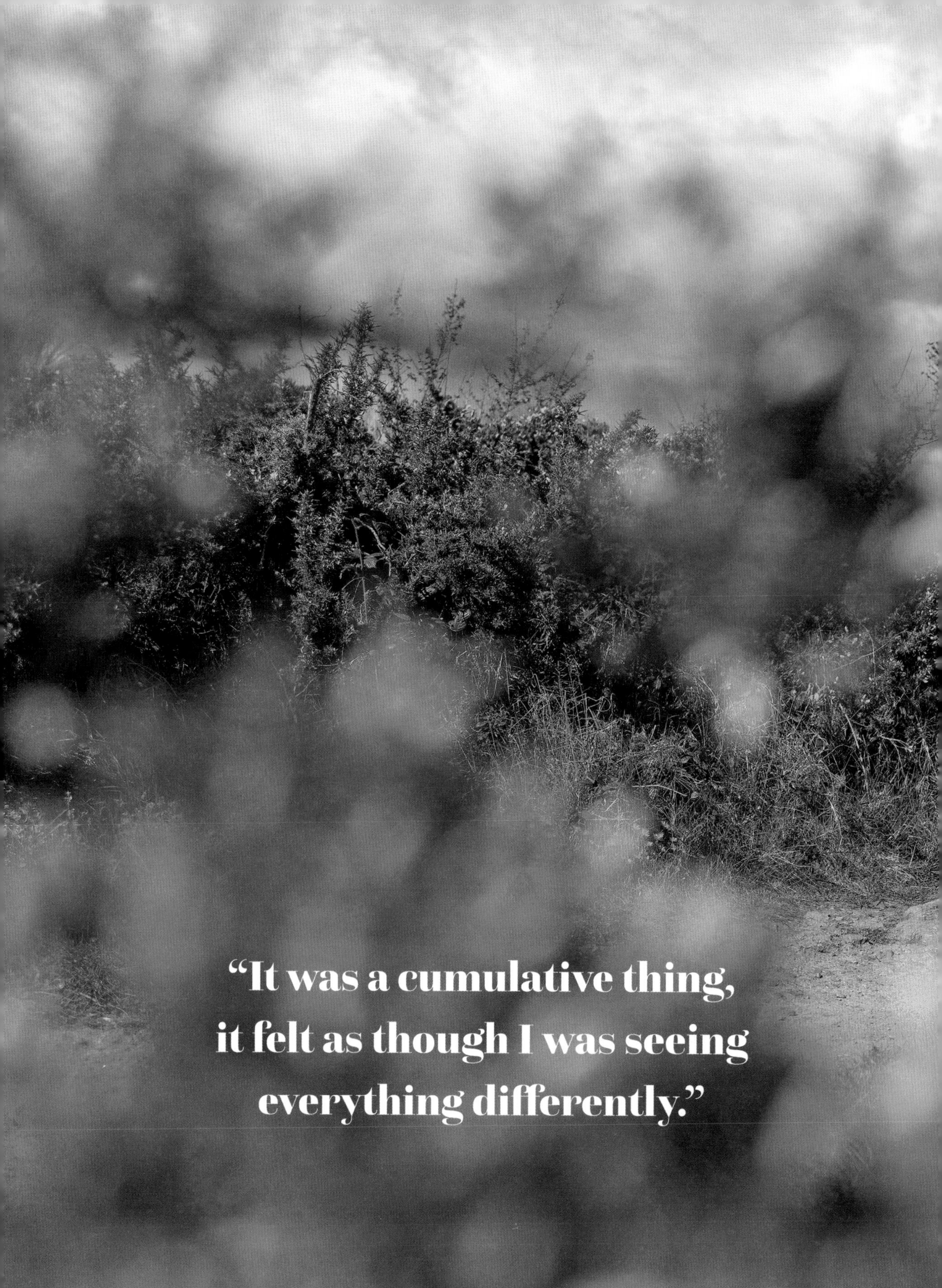
"It was a cumulative thing,
it felt as though I was seeing
everything differently."

MARTY MORRISSEY

THE GAP OF DUNLOE

MARTY MORRISSEY was born in Mallow and entered the world of broadcasting in 1988, becoming well known and loved in Ireland for presenting high-profile sports events such as the Olympics, GAA Games, Pro Box Live and Saturday Sport on RTÉ Radio 1 and commentating on the All Ireland Finals on TV and Radio. He traded the sports pitch for the ballroom dancefloor in 2018 as he took part in RTÉ's *Dancing with the Stars* and released his autobiography *It's Marty* in 2022, donating the proceeds of the book launch to the Irish Emergency Alliance Ukraine Appeal to help those displaced by the conflict.

Fifteen minutes' drive from Killarney, in Co. Kerry, the Gap of Dunloe is a narrow mountain pass forged by glaciers. Set between the MacGillycuddy Reeks and Purple Mountain, the landscape is rich and varied, with lakes, waterfalls and lush green scenery. Best explored on bicycle, by foot or by jaunting car, the traditional pony and traps operated by horsemen known locally as jarveys. The clip-clop sounds of ponies in the distance is just one of the reasons why Marty Morrissey selected the Gap of Dunloe as his perfect place . . .

It's the smells and the sounds of the horses that captivate me. The sound of their grunting and heavy breathing, and strange as it may sound, the smell of horse manure all along the Gap of Dunloe. It is so wholesome and it takes me back.

I was brought up in New York until I was ten years old but we used to go home to Ireland on holidays to my grandfather's farm in West Clare. He had a big grey mare called Fanny. As a child I'd hear Fanny coming along the road, the clip-clop of her hooves, a sound you don't hear so much anymore. I was brought to the Gap of Dunloe for the first time on those holidays. And it's that sound, the clip-clopping of the ponies and the lilting Kerry tones of the jarveys – "Come on boy, come on" – that brings me back to my childhood and does my heart good.

I don't go through the gap by jaunting car, although the jarvey lads will sometimes offer me a lift. I like to walk, often with my partner Liz, just taking it all in. It's one of those iconic places in Ireland and

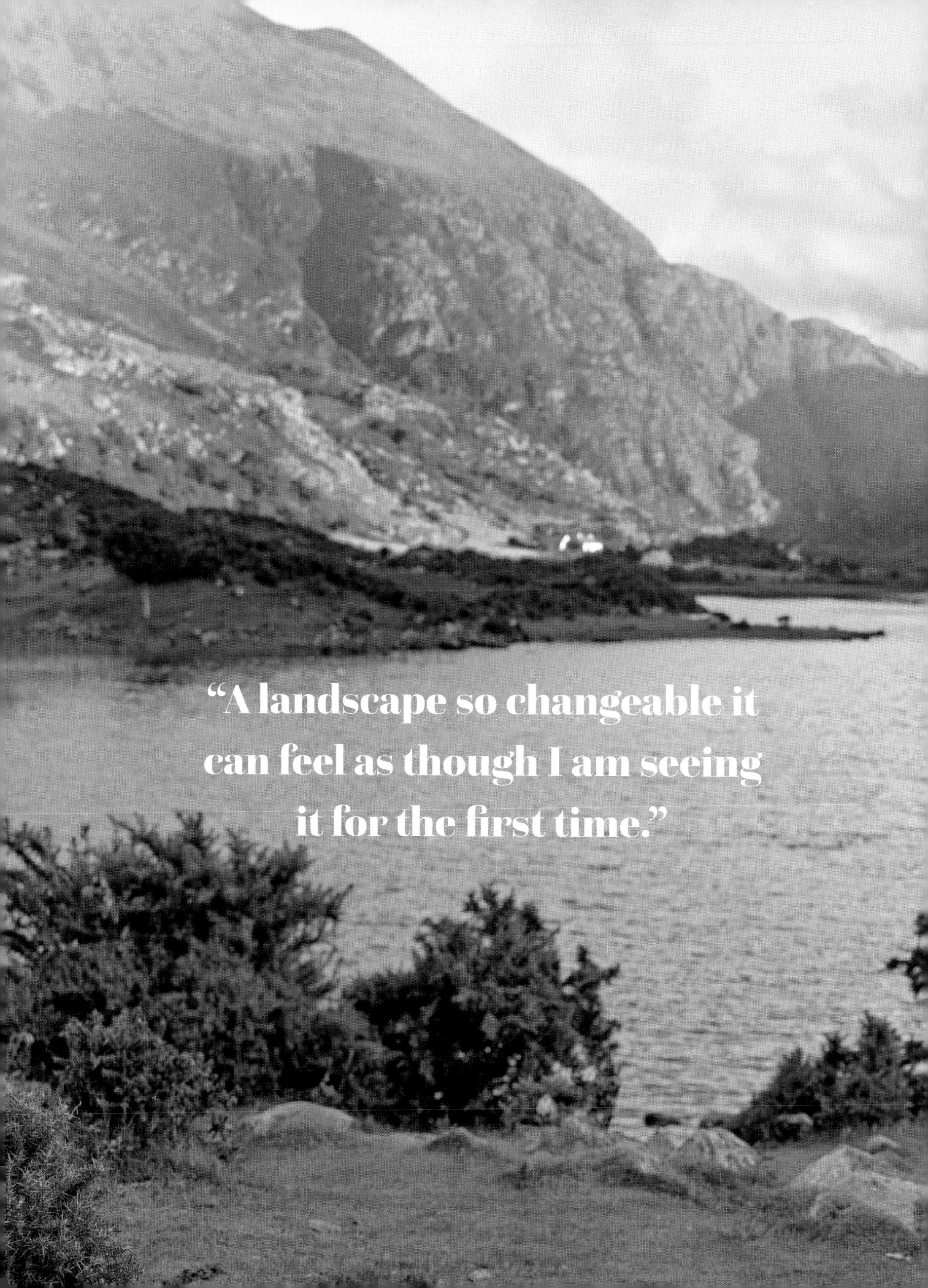
"A landscape so changeable it can feel as though I am seeing it for the first time."

"Kerry also gives me a sense of pride of how beautiful our country is, whether it's Kenmare or Killarney or Dingle."

the beauty of the place kind of symbolises everything that is great about our country. It feels so familiar, like a movie version of Ireland, but this is not a movie, it's real. All you can do is marvel.

Cars can go through the gap, but not many do and I'm glad it's a mostly car-free zone. The entire walk is around 11km, a grand stretch from the famous Kate Kearney's Cottage where many people begin their journey.

The original Kate Kearney was apparently a great beauty before the famine times, and ran a sibín here. This is where she distilled her poitín which was known as Kate Kearney's Mountain Dew. It's said that it was as lethal as it was illegal – "very fierce and wild, requiring not less than seven times its own quantity of water to tame and subdue it."

There's even a song about her. She sounded like a formidable woman altogether:

Oh! Have you not heard of Kate Kearney,
Who lives on the banks of Killarney;
From the glance of her eye,
Shun danger and fly,
For fatal's the glance of Kate Kearney

The walk takes you past five gorgeous lakes in total. On each side, there are those majestic mountains, and up on the ridges you can see sheep. I often think, "How are they surviving up there?" There are also ruins along the way, remnants of homes dating back to the famine years.

It's a meandering, exhilarating walk. The path climbs up and back down again through a landscape so changeable it can feel as though I am seeing it for the first time. My favourite part is when the gap gets very narrow, up past the arched stone bridge which is known as the Wishing Bridge, between Coosaun Lough and Black Lake. If you make a wish when you cross this bridge over the River Loe, it's certain to come true. That's what they tell me anyway.

The walk takes you all the way down the twisty road to Lord Brandon's Cottage in the Black Valley where you can get a nice bowl of hot soup after all your endeavours and from there, if you fancy it, take a boat across the lakes to Ross Castle just outside Killarney.

Being from the neighbouring county of Clare, I've always had an affection for

Kerry. I admire their footballing skills of course but Kerry also gives me a sense of pride of how beautiful our country is, whether it's Kenmare or Killarney or Dingle. But I'm probably fondest of the Gap of Dunloe, especially in wintertime when it's not so busy and the serenity of the landscape is almost overwhelming. I don't think there's any place like it. I always say if I am ever missing, that's where you will most likely find me. It's heaven on earth.

Penfield

MARTIN "BEANZ" WARDE

GALWAY

Martin Warde is a stand-up comedian, writer and podcaster with a passion for telling stories from the margins. Martin writes for *The Irish Times* and *Irish Examiner*, and is a regular on TV panels on RTÉ and Virgin Media, alongside his own podcast the *HazBeanz* show. He is currently writing his first play, *The Dead House*, and working on projects with the National Museum of Ireland and Photo Museum of Ireland that respectively aim to archive Traveller oral history from the community's elders and explore perspective and expressionism within the Traveller community.

Known as the City of the Tribes, Galway is situated in the west of Ireland on the River Corrib, a few minutes' drive from the Atlantic Ocean. With an arty, bohemian atmosphere, winding streets, legendary pubs and traditional music on almost every corner, the medieval city is a mecca for tourists, a youthful place full of festivals, fun and stories. Galway city is also a gateway to some of the most scenic locations in that county, including Lough Corrib and the Connemara wilderness, locations that mean a lot to Martin "Beanz" Warde, who says Galway is his perfect place in Ireland . . .

To tell the story of why Galway is my perfect place, I have to go back a bit. Growing up, my family lived in tents, cooking and sleeping in tarpaulins thrown over a stone wall. That was a tough existence, not a lifestyle to be romanticised. When I was very young we would have travelled around Ireland in a caravan, with cousins who were my closest friends, not living in any one fixed place. We stopped travelling when we got to Athenry, Co. Galway, the place where my mother and granny were from.

After that we moved into a house on a council estate in Tuam, Co. Galway. That's where my relationship with the county really began. Moving into a house was a game changer but not necessarily in a positive way. For the first while I remember

Head
Galway
Gaillimh
Irish 'Pub of the Year' 1651

feeling almost caged. But my parents had sacrificed their traditional Travelling lives and culture for stable living, for us to have a better future and a good education.

It wasn't until I went to school in Tuam that I began to realise I was being treated differently because of my background. It was the way teachers put all the Traveller kids together on one desk, how they overpoliced us or asked questions about whether our parents were feeding us. I was put into remedial classes that I shouldn't have been in. We were extremely wise to it as kids.

The impact of all of this was profound. At about eleven or twelve, I started writing poetry and voicing it in what I thought was a settled person's accent. I was consciously trying to get rid of the accent I had picked up from travelling around the country. I wasn't turning away from Traveller culture, I was turning away from what I saw as the weakness and vulnerability that came with it, giving myself armour to go out into the world.

I had one good teacher in school who told me to remember that it wasn't about where I came from but where I was going that really mattered. It took a while but I started to take pride in Tuam. There was so much to be proud of, from playwright Tom Murphy to the Saw Doctors. And while the bullying and discrimination I experienced at school wasn't right, it did create a deep empathy in me for others who are treated badly.

At eighteen I did an Access course to try and get into college. That's when I went off to Galway city for the first time. I always remember going up there from Tuam, eyes wide open, making new friends at house parties, getting served alcohol in a club. I was flabbergasted. I started doing comedy after being chosen as a participant in the TV show *Joy in Da Hood*. It wasn't until 2009 that I eventually got around to doing my arts degree at the National University of Ireland, Galway. It took a while because there was a death in our family and various other interruptions to my studies, but I finally got my degree in 2015. I didn't actually get conferred, because at the time I couldn't afford the gown and I didn't want to be the only one without robes in the photographs.

I came out as a gay man at an LGBTQ+ event during Galway Pride in 2016. Galway is a great place to be gay. Obviously, you are going to meet nasty people everywhere, the kind who say horrible things about everyone from women to trans people. For the most part Galway is a place where you can just be yourself. I have drag queen friends who walk down the streets of Galway with not a bother on them. You'd see these guys, football supporters in their jerseys, asking them for selfies.

Everything blossomed for me after I came out. I started getting into photography and noticing nature, which led to me discovering the beauty of Galway beyond the city. It was as though, by finally owning my own true identity not just as a Travel-

“When I go on jaunts around Galway there always seems to be someone to show you around.”

Teach Tábhairne
agus Bialann

ler but as a gay man, a weight was lifted off my shoulders. I could see the beauty of everything around me rather than focusing on the fear that had weighed me down before.

I went to Lough Corrib for the first time and fell in love with the place. Some people will say it's nothing special but it's special to me. You drive into Oughterard, with the lovely shops and pubs, then over this stone bridge where there are brown trout swimming in the water. You go up a gorgeous hill, look out over the hundreds of islands on the lake (which is the second largest in Ireland) and reach this viewing point; it's all wild sheep and mountains and that powerful, intoxicatingly sweet smell of hawthorn.

I've been there many times since, but I remember the first time I went down to the crumbling stone pier near the viewing point. I sat there just listening to the

“It’s all wild sheep and mountains and that powerful, intoxicatingly sweet smell of hawthorn.”

lapping of the water, so rhythmic and calming. I put my feet into the water and noticed how lake water feels softer on the skin than the sea.

It was whilst sitting on that pier that I realised I needed to see more of the county. I also connected with the part of me that was lost when my family stopped travelling. I wanted to know what was beyond Oughterard. I went to Rosmuc. To Renvyle. I explored all over Connemara. I went to Dog’s Bay and Roundstone. And everywhere there were people issuing magical directions, “Go on up the road there, jump over the gate, past the field with the two horses, wait until you see.” I’d follow their instructions and find a hidden pond or some other Galway secret spot, a fairy fort from the road, maybe. When I go on jaunts around Galway there always seems to be someone to show you around and share their passion for the place.

I’ve discovered the county more in recent years, but I love Galway city still. It’s a bohemian place full of hippies where everyone has their quirks and there’s always a smell of weed in the air. People are going around wearing homemade jumpers and recycled sandals and everyone is trying to outdo each other by being more vegan than the next vegan. For me, it’s the simple things. Having a few pints in the King’s Head, a beautiful pub which I performed in for the Galway Arts festival and serves the finest fish and chips in the area.

What I love most about Galway is that it feels like home. Walking down the streets, I might meet ten people I know in the space of half an hour, which is something you don’t get in larger cities. We still do that thing of saying hello to strangers on the streets. It’s the nod of the head, or a smile as they walk past.

There are still so many places around the county I’m dying to explore. I want to go out to the Aran Islands and up to Letterfrack and Glenlo Abbey. In a way I’m still on a journey of discovery with Galway, a journey that began when I was a small child in Tuam. I can’t wait to see what I discover next.

ACKNOWLEDGEMENTS

Thanks to everyone who spoke to me for this book, to Sean Cahill, who captured these extraordinary places, and to A Lust for Life, for the brilliant work you do.

A big thanks to Simon Hess, who put me in touch with my publisher. It was a joy to work with Black & White Publishing, especially with Rachel Morrell, the most patient, tenacious and talented editor a writer could hope for. Thanks for everything, Rach. Also to my agent Faith O'Grady and all at the Lisa Richards Agency.

To Anna Cosgrave, Alex Clark and Danny Kelly, who know frazzled writers need the finest boltholes when those final deadlines loom – thank you all so much for having me. Thanks to Jonathan Hobson for your exceptional copy-editing skills. And to Jonny, Joya and Priya: thanks as always for putting up with me. You are my other perfect place.

RÓISÍN INGLE is a journalist and podcaster with *The Irish Times*. She is co-presenter and producer of the award-winning Women's Podcast and her popular weekly columns have been collected in two books, *Pieces of Me* and *Public Displays of Emotion*. She is the author, with Natasha Fennell, of Irish bestseller *The Daughterhood* which explored mother-daughter relationships. Róisín lives in Dublin with her partner and twin teenage daughters. You'll find her on Twitter and Instagram @roisiningle